I0817262

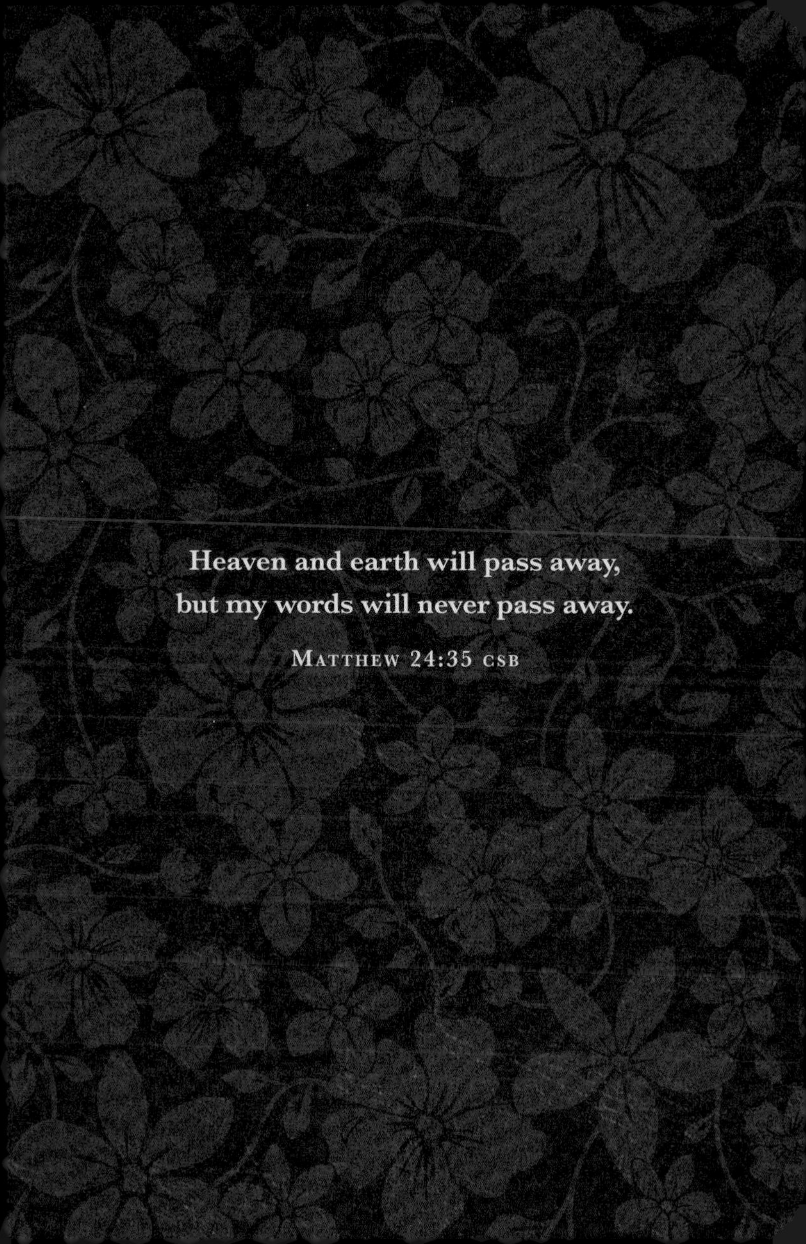

Heaven and earth will pass away,
but my words will never pass away.

Matthew 24:35 csb

Introduction

Do you long for a deeper connection with God and a greater understanding of his Word? *The Bible Reading Plan Devotional for Women* is designed to guide you through the entire Bible in one year.

Each entry includes carefully selected passages of Scripture, insightful meditations that bring biblical truths to life, and heartfelt prayers to help draw you closer to God and seek his wisdom in all areas of your life. Whether you're new to Bible reading or have been studying for years, this devotional will equip you to stay consistent, deepen your faith, and discover the transformative power of God's Word.

Open these pages and experience the beauty of walking through the Bible one day at a time. Let this year be the year you grow in faith, wisdom, and intimacy with your Creator.

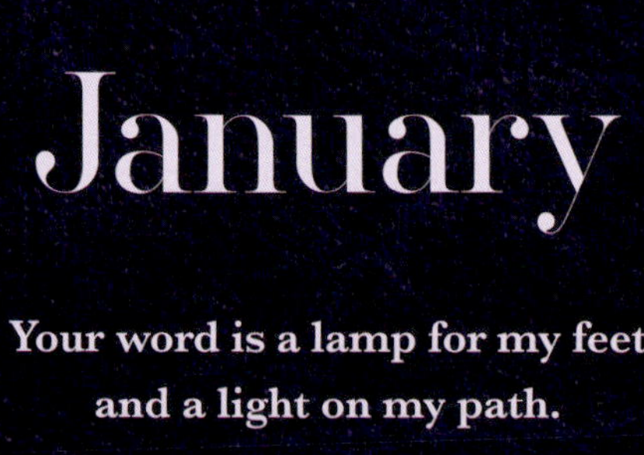

January

Your word is a lamp for my feet
and a light on my path.

Psalm 119:105 CSB

Scripture Reading: Genesis 1-3

Created in Goodness

God saw all that he had made, and it was very good.
GENESIS 1:31 NIV

When God created the world and everything in it, he wasn't just satisfied. He determined that what he had made was *very good*. At the end of the sixth day, God sat back and took his creation in. Everything was good, from the seas and mountains to the animals of the earth and sky. But this is not all that God declared good. Humanity was born of God's heart. It was created with love, and it was *very good* in his eyes.

When you question your worth, remember who made you. God doesn't make mistakes! He is full of love for you, and he longs for you to come alive in his kindness. You might look around and see a lack of goodness in the world. Ask God to reveal his everlasting mercy to you, to see where his goodness still stands.

Creator, when I struggle to see goodness in others and in myself, show me where the light of your love breaks through. I look to you.

Scripture Reading: Genesis 4-6

Made in His Image

This is the written account of the descendants of Adam. When God created human beings, he made them to be like himself.

GENESIS 5:1 NLT

God created humans to be like himself. So, when we look at the character of God, we can more fully understand what he wants us to be like. God, the merciful one, has not changed a bit over time. Therefore, as we look at the rest of his Word and how he meets his people throughout the ages, we can recognize his unflinching nature shining through.

Galatians 5:22-23 explains the fruit of God's Spirit: his divine imprint. This is as good a place to begin as any other. Jesus, the living embodiment of God's nature is our guiding light and source, and he exemplified the Spirit's fruit perfectly.

Lord, I want to be more like you. Help me to live out your fruit in my life and in my choices. I choose to follow your ways.

Scripture Reading: Genesis 7-9

Signs of Promise

"When the bow is in the clouds, I will see it and remember the everlasting covenant between God and every living creature of all flesh that is on the earth."

GENESIS 9:16 ESV

Rainbows serve to remind us of God's promise to creation. The great flood will never be repeated. Nature's signs can also encourage us to remember the sovereignty of God in our daily lives. The sparrows find their food, and bees nourish in the flowerbeds. We too will be taken care of and provided for by the Creator of all living things.

Perhaps you have experienced deliverance or a promise from the Lord that he has kept faithfully. What sign can point your attention back to his faithfulness? It can be something closely linked or a seemingly random cue. Ask the Holy Spirit to give you a sign, a codeword, to remind you of his covenant with you.

God, thank you for your faithful love and your promises that never fail. Deepen my trust as you remind me of all that you have done in my life.

Scripture Reading: Genesis 10-12

Courage to Trust

"I will make you into a great nation,
I will bless you,
I will make your name great,
and you will be a blessing."
GENESIS 12:2 CSB

God spoke to Abram, instructing him to leave his homeland and everything he knew well. God did not stop with that command though. He gave him a promise to hold onto, a reason to follow the leading of the Lord. That promise is found in today's Scripture.

When God instructs us to follow him, he also gives us his promise. Abram was obedient to God, and his faith was credited to him as righteousness (Hebrews 11). When we walk in obedience, we can be sure that God goes with us. We can trust his leadership, and we can trust his power. He is able to do what no one else can. He will powerfully reveal his faithfulness as we partner with him.

Lord, you are my strength. Remind me how great you are when I waver in obedience. May my trust go deep in the truth of who you were, are, and always will be.

Scripture Reading: Genesis 13-15

Heirs of Promise

He took him outside and said, "Now look toward the heavens and count the stars, if you are able to count them." And He said to him, "So shall your descendants be."

GENESIS 15:5 NASB

Have you ever considered that *you* are a part of the promise God made to Abraham? The stars in the sky can't be counted: they are too great in number! That is what God used to compare the people of his kingdom, the descendants that would come through Abraham.

When God makes a promise, he will never break it. We are descendants of the promise through Christ, and we are also co-heirs with him (Romans 8:17). What God does, he does exceedingly well. Sometimes the very perspective shift we need in faith is to remember that God is at work faithfully fulfilling his promises, and our part is simple obedience.

Father, thank you for the power of your faithfulness. You weave together what we don't consider. Have your way in my life, and help me to trust you fully with every part of it.

Scripture Reading: Genesis 16-18

The God Who Sees

Then she called the name of the LORD who spoke to her, You-Are-the-God-Who-Sees; for she said, "Have I also here seen Him who sees me?"

GENESIS 16:13 NKJV

While our tendency may be to overlook those who don't fit our preferred narrative, God does not play favorites. He is the God who sees. He sees the outcast, the vulnerable, and the scapegoat. He draws near to all who draw near to him.

Hagar was put in the position she was in by her mistress and master. Sarah and Abraham were the ones who initially chose this path of action. Let's remember to check our biases when we begin to judge others rather than extend them grace and mercy. God saw. He knew. He honored. Let's join his heart and do the same with the overlooked among us.

God, you see and know the truth of every heart and the origin of every hardship. Melt my heart in your love and give me eyes of grace and compassion.

Scripture Reading: Genesis 19-21

Release Control

The Lord cared for Sarah as he had said and did for her what he had promised. Sarah became pregnant and gave birth to a son for Abraham in his old age. Everything happened at the time God had said it would.

Genesis 21:1-2 NCV

Remember how Sarah tried to fulfill God's promise? She couldn't believe that her body would be able to bear a child, so she took things into her own hands. That didn't work out so well for her, did it? And what did God do? He faithfully fulfilled his Word!

God will do what he has promised, and we don't have to try to control it. In fact, the more we surrender in trust, the freer we will be in faith. Let's give up the need to make things happen and let them unfold as they will. God is faithful. He will do it!

Lord, you were faithful to Sarah, even when she struggled to believe that you could do what you promised. Give me greater faith to surrender my hopes to you. I trust your timing and ability.

Scripture Reading: Genesis 22-24

Response of Praise

Then the man bowed down and worshiped the LORD, saying, "Praise be to the LORD, the God of my master Abraham, who has not abandoned his kindness and faithfulness to my master. As for me, the LORD has led me on the journey to the house of my master's relatives."

GENESIS 24:26-27 NIV

When God answers our prayers, it is a rightful response to praise him. Abraham's servant went out under Abraham's direction to find a wife for Isaac. He prayed, asking the Lord to reveal his choice through a specific set of circumstances. God answered that prayer, and the man's response was praise.

We don't have to be afraid to pray in very specific ways. When God answers us, our gratitude will come pouring out in praise. God is still full of kindness and faithfulness toward his people. Let's trust him to guide us in every matter.

Lord God, you are the faithful one from the beginning. You are still faithful today. I offer you my trust and ask for your hand to guide me clearly. Thank you.

Scripture Reading: Genesis 25-27

Reassurance

"I am the God of your father, Abraham," he said. "Do not be afraid, for I am with you and will bless you. I will multiply your descendants, and they will become a great nation. I will do this because of my promise to Abraham, my servant."

GENESIS 26:24 NLT

God reminds us of who he is so we will trust him with our hearts and lives. Isaac was in a new land, a place where the Lord told him to settle, and God's favor is what turned the hearts of the people toward him in peace.

When God gives us direction, we might face resistance from others. But we are to take God at his Word and follow him. He faithfully follows through on his promises, and he will not fail. The more we trust him, the less it matters what others think. He knows us well, and he knows our weakness. He offers reassurance right when we need it.

Father, you are the God of Abraham and Isaac, but you are also my God. Speak to me today and lead me in love. I will follow you.

Scripture Reading: Genesis 28-30

Wherever You Go

"Behold, I am with you and will keep you wherever you go, and will bring you back to this land. For I will not leave you until I have done what I have promised you."

Genesis 28:15 ESV

God's presence is our greatest assurance. He is with us, and he goes where we go. The psalmist said it this way: "Where shall I go from your Spirit? Or where shall I flee from your presence? If I ascend to heaven you are there! If I make my bed in Sheol, you are there!" (Psalm 139:7-8). We cannot escape him, and that is very good news.

Just as God promised to be with Jacob wherever he went, so he promises to be with all his people. Jacob's response to God's promise was to commit himself to the Lord. Have you taken the Lord up on his promise? Have you offered him your devotion?

Lord, it is unimaginable the lengths you go to show your love. I want to know you more, to see your hand guiding me in truth and in power. You are mine, and I am yours wherever I go.

Scripture Reading: Genesis 31-33

A New Name

"Your name will no longer be Jacob," he said. "It will be Israel because you have struggled with God and with men and have prevailed."

Genesis 32:28 CSB

There is a special level of honor that comes from wrestling in faith with God. He does not demand blind allegiance. He delights when we engage him with passion and curiosity. Though we may think he wants us to be unquestioning, that is not true at all!

God can handle your true longings and questions. Jacob wrestled with the angel of the Lord and would not give up until he received a blessing. When you have the audacity to not simply settle for what is offered and let your passion drive you to God for more, the result is a new identity and a blessing.

God, I am not satisfied with the little I have known of you. I want to know you more! May I have the boldness of Jacob and not relent in your presence.

Scripture Reading: Genesis 34-36

House of God

Jacob named the place where God had spoken with him, Bethel.

GENESIS 35:15 NASB

The Hebrew word Bethel means "house of God." It is a holy place. This makes sense when we consider how Jacob named the place where God spoke with him *Bethel*. It was holy ground, a sacred space.

The New Testament reveals that God's home is not in a sanctuary; God has chosen to make his home in his people (Hebrews 3:6; Ephesians 3:17). If the Spirit resides in us, then that means the Word of the Lord is living and active within us. Our hearts and lives become the place where God speaks. From deep to deep, we receive the Word of the Lord within our spirits.

Lord, I want to live with the awareness that I am a walking, talking house of your presence. Speak to me today, and I will live. May your Word come alive in me as you offer the revelation of your wisdom through your Spirit.

Scripture Reading: Genesis 37-39

Ever-Present Help

He was there in the prison. But the LORD was with Joseph and showed him mercy, and He gave him favor in the sight of the keeper of the prison.

GENESIS 39:20-21 NKJV

Joseph did not have an easy life. He was dearly loved by his parents, but his brothers put him through a lot, including selling him off to get rid of him. Can you imagine what that was like? Joseph had an inspiring dream and shared it with his brothers, but they let bitterness guide their actions instead of grace.

It didn't matter what Joseph went through. God was with him through it all. He gave him favor with his master, until he turned against him at his wife's lies. In the prison system, Joseph also found favor with the head guard. Eventually this favor would lead Joseph to live out his dreams. If you've encountered trials and think God has lost track of where he was leading you, take heart from Joseph's story. He isn't finished with you yet!

Lord, you are the ultimate promise keeper, and you haven't forgotten what you began in me. I trust you.

Scripture Reading: Genesis 40-42

Wisdom and Understanding

The king said to Joseph, "God has shown you all this. There is no one as wise and understanding as you are, so I will put you in charge of my palace. All the people will obey your orders, and only I will be greater than you."

GENESIS 41:39-40 NCV

Wisdom and understanding lead to honor. Joseph remained submitted to the Lord, no matter the injustice of his circumstances. He did not let his trials lead him to bitterness. He continued to work at all he was offered with integrity and honor. In turn, he was honored.

Your character matters more than notoriety. If you are trustworthy, you will be offered more responsibility. Work at what you have with all your heart, and trust God's timing when it comes to bringing favor and opportunities. He will give you wisdom and understanding as you humbly follow him.

Lord, I want to cultivate a character of gold, where your wisdom and understanding matter more to me than the treasures of this world.

Scripture Reading: Genesis 43-45

Mercy Matters

Joseph said to his brothers, "I am Joseph! Is my father still living?" But his brothers were not able to answer him, because they were terrified at his presence.

GENESIS 45:3 NIV

When Joseph revealed himself to his brothers, he did not rub his authority in their faces. He didn't yell at them or demand them to bow down before him. His first question was about their father. The brothers experienced a very different reaction. They were terrified.

Joseph's continued response is more than gracious. It is a beautiful picture of God's mercy. He assured his brothers that he was sent ahead in order to preserve his people through the authority that had been given him. He not only gave them a fresh start, he also gave them a higher perspective, releasing them from guilt and shame. Let's lead with mercy and allow the Lord to work through even the things that others mean for evil.

God, I want to be as merciful with those who have hurt me. I don't want to drown in bitterness. Give me a fresh outlook and help me to live in gracious forgiveness.

Scripture Reading: Genesis 46-48

A Promise Fulfilled

"I am God, the God of your father," the voice said. "Do not be afraid to go down to Egypt, for there I will make your family into a great nation. I will go with you down to Egypt, and I will bring you back again."

GENESIS 46:3-4 NLT

God promised Jacob that if he went down to Egypt with his sons, Joseph would be with him at the end of his life. He took all he had and brought his family to where God directed him. Joseph was in a place of authority in Egypt where he could protect and provide for his father. It was God's grace that he used what was meant for evil as good.

God is still in the business of turning bad situations into opportunities for his faithfulness to shine. What he has started, he is still doing. Don't lose heart if you are unsure how God will meet you in the messes of life. He not only will meet you, he will also provide a way through.

God, be with me now, and show me the way through the trials of life. I trust you.

Scripture Reading: Genesis 49-50

Release Control

Joseph said to them, "Do not fear, for am I in the place of God? As for you, you meant evil against me, but God meant it for good, to bring it about that many people should be kept alive, as they are today."

GENESIS 50:19-20 ESV

It is not our job to judge others. We think we can punish others, and it will feel satisfying. The truth is the only satisfaction is in the freedom of God's love, his salvation, and his grace. When we humble ourselves and leave the rest to God, we have no need to control the narrative.

Even what was intended to harm us can be turned around for good. God does not cause us harm, but he can coordinate the fruit of his goodness out of absolutely any situation.

Lord, I let go of the need to retaliate against others, and I choose to trust your goodness to win in the end. You are greater than my pain, and your heart is generous in redemptive power.

Scripture Reading: Exodus 1-3

A Remarkable Sight

Then the angel of the LORD appeared to him in a flame of fire within a bush. As Moses looked, he saw that the bush was on fire but was not consumed. When the LORD saw that he had gone over to look, God called out to him from the bush, "Moses, Moses!"

EXODUS 3:2,4 CSB

Sometimes God meets us in unexpected ways. Moses' attention was caught by a flame of fire in a bush that wasn't destructive. It boggled his mind so much that he had to take a closer look. When he approached the remarkable sight, God called his name.

We are often so busy going about our lives that we miss out on our surroundings. Instead of being consumed with technology, let's leave room in our hearts and minds for curiosity. Let's pay attention so that when the unexpected occurs, we can lean in and hear God's voice.

Father, I don't want to be so busy that I miss your bid for my attention. Open my heart and mind to connect with you in the world around me.

Scripture Reading: Exodus 4-6

Equipped

The LORD said to him, "Who has made the human mouth? Or who makes anyone unable to speak or deaf, or able to see or blind? Is it not I, the LORD? Now then go, and I Myself will be with your mouth, and instruct you in what you are to say."

EXODUS 4:11-12 NASB

Do you ever wonder how God could use you? Even the fathers of the faith had insecurities. Moses tried to tell God why he wasn't the right candidate for speaking. He explained that he had never been eloquent. Who would listen to him or take him seriously?

God doesn't need our ability. He wants our willingness. He can bless and use what we deem insignificant and faulty. He is the one who made us as we are, and he knows what he's doing when he calls us. If you feel ill-equipped to do what God is leading you to do, that's good news! He can move through you in greater ways when you rely on him.

God, I know that you are with me in all that you are leading me into. Instruct me, and I will follow.

Scripture Reading: Exodus 7-9

Trust and Obey

Moses and Aaron did so; just as the Lord commanded them, so they did.

Exodus 7:6 NKJV

God was with Moses and Aaron in all that he instructed them to do. When they went before Pharoah, God put power behind their words. They believed God wanted freedom for his people, and followed his direction for what to say and do. They trusted him and obeyed, and we know what happened next.

When we put our trust in God, let's not leave it at wishful thinking. If he has given us a clear step to take, we must take it. If he has told us to wait, it's important that we trust his timing. If he has shown us the people to connect with, let's show up and connect with them. He knows what he is doing.

Lord, you are the same God who instructed Moses and Aaron, and I will not let trust remain a theory. When you speak, I will listen. When you lead me, I will follow.

Scripture Reading: Exodus 10-12

New Beginnings

The LORD spoke to Moses and Aaron in the land of Egypt: "This month will be the beginning of months, the first month of the year for you."

EXODUS 12:1-2 NCV

God created a new beginning for his people in Egypt. At the first Passover, they had to trust God in a way they hadn't before. This would be the beginning of their liberation from Egypt. To this day, Passover remains a time of remembrance for God's people.

When God offers us new beginnings, it is often out of the destruction of old ways. We cannot stay in our Egypt and experience the freedom he calls us into. We have to be willing to follow him out into the wilderness and to trust him to provide for us in ways we haven't had to before. He is faithful, and he knows what he is doing.

God, my flesh wants to stay comfortable in what is known, while my soul longs for the freedom you promise. Help me to choose you and to trust you.

Scripture Reading: Exodus 13-15

Stand Firm

Moses answered the people, "Do not be afraid. Stand firm and you will see the deliverance the LORD will bring you today. The Egyptians you see today you will never see again. The LORD will fight for you; you need only to be still."

EXODUS 14:13-14 NIV

The fears of the Israelites were heightened as they caught sight of the Egyptians marching after them. They were panicking; they thought they would surely die. Regret and panic mingled together. Did this stop God from faithfully following through? By no means!

When you can't see a way out of a chaotic situation, don't give up hope. Don't go back to how things were. You haven't come this far just to give in to fear. Dig in your heels. Stand firm, and you will see the deliverance of the Lord. He does not lead you to abandon you.

Lord, when fear rises in me and panic settles into my chest, remind me of how powerful and near you are. Your presence is my lifeline!

Scripture Reading: Exodus 16-18

Provision

The Israelites were puzzled when they saw it. "What is it?" they asked each other. They had no idea what it was. And Moses told them, "It is the food the LORD has given you to eat."

EXODUS 16:15 NLT

Provision doesn't always appear how we expect, but it always meets our need. Just because we don't recognize the use of something at first does not mean it is useless. God's provision is sufficient, and he is endlessly creative. Let's not give up hope because we fail to recognize his goodness.

With open eyes, open hearts, and grateful hands, let's receive what God offers us today. We can trust his provision, for he never fails. When it comes in ways we did not anticipate, let us not hesitate in receiving it, for his gifts are always good. Let's allow him to broaden our understanding and our expectation as he continually provides for our needs.

Father, I don't want to reject your provision because it comes in a way I did not expect. I humble my heart to receive your gifts of goodness with gratitude.

Scripture Reading: Exodus 19-21

Remember

"You yourselves have seen what I did to the Egyptians, and how I bore you on eagles' wings and brought you to myself."

Exodus 19:4 ESV

God led his people out of their captivity, and it wasn't so that they would get lost in the desert. He brought them out of Egypt to experience his leadership. Before Moses went up on Mount Sinai to meet face-to-face with the Lord, the people were encouraged to remember God's power.

God's rescue is tender. It's not about showing you what he can do for power's sake but because of his love for you. He wants you near for your sake. He wants you to know him in power, in truth, and in love.

Lord, you are the God who brings us to yourself. I want to know the power of your presence, the incomparable confidence of your kindness, and the liberation of your leadership.

Scripture Reading: Exodus 22-25

Called In

"You must not exploit a resident alien or oppress him, since you were resident aliens in the land of Egypt."

Exodus 22:21 csb

God's Word is clear. He welcomes the stranger and the outcast. He watches over the vulnerable and oppressed. There is no one out of reach from his love. He covers the entire world with his redemptive kindness, and he gladly welcomes all who turn to him as his own. God never forgets the outsider.

It is human nature to repeat what we've experienced, but God calls us to a higher way: a supernatural love. We were all outsiders in some capacity before we found ourselves at home in Christ. God's kingdom is not exclusive. Let's follow in his footsteps and take his Word seriously as we live it out in our communities.

God, may I never forget how kind, generous, and inclusive you are. You love me well, and I want to love others well too.

Scripture Reading: Exodus 26-28

Most Holy Place

"You shall hang up the veil under the clasps, and bring in the ark of the testimony there within the veil; and the veil shall serve as a partition for you between the Holy Place and the Most Holy Place."

Exodus 26:33 NASB

God determined to dwell with his people. He instructed them how to build a tabernacle that included a place for him at the center—the Holy of Holies. It was a thick veil that separated the presence of God from the rest of the tabernacle.

When Jesus died on the cross, it is that same veil, that separated God's presence from the people, that was torn. We are living temples of the Holy Spirit, able to access him anywhere without hesitation through Christ. This is exceedingly good news! The yielded hearts of God's people have become the Most Holy Place.

Spirit of God, you are welcome here in my heart and life. Thank you for the power of your Spirit that teaches, guides, and corrects me.

Scripture Reading: Exodus 29-31

Spirit of Creativity

"I have filled him with the Spirit of God, in wisdom, in understanding, in knowledge, and in all manner of workmanship, to design artistic works, to work in gold, in silver, in bronze, in cutting jewels for setting, in carving wood, and to work in all manner of workmanship."

EXODUS 31:3-5 NKJV

Creativity is a gift from God. Skilled craftmanship reflects the handiwork and skill of our great Maker. The same God who made the mountains, starry host, and each of us is the one who gifts us with talents.

We were created to do more than work. We were made to create: to use our imaginations, skills, and playful curiosity to artfully birth new expressions of ancient ideas. We are unique. Our thoughts, voices, and contributions are special. Let's use our authentic innovation to glorify the Lord.

Lord, I don't want to become so serious that I forget there is an element of imagination and play that go into building skills. Thank you for your gift of creativity.

Scripture Reading: Exodus 32-34

Like a Friend

The LORD spoke to Moses face to face as a man speaks with his friend.

EXODUS 33:11 NCV

Moses' relationship with God wasn't formal. Although he surely honored the Lord and was well-acquainted with his power, he still spoke to the Lord as friends do. He got right in the presence of God and not only listened to what the Lord said but talked to him as well.

God doesn't need our formality. He wants us to know him so closely that others will be able to tell we were in his presence by the light shining on our faces. Let's go to the Lord as often as possible in our hearts and minds through prayer. We don't have to wait another moment to know him in Spirit and in truth, or to speak to him as a friend.

Lord, I don't want to wonder about you, I want to know you. I come to you as a friend today, opening my heart to you.

Scripture Reading: Exodus 35-37

Movement of the Heart

Everyone who was willing and whose heart moved them came and brought an offering to the LORD for the work on the tent of meeting, for all its service, and for the sacred garments.

EXODUS 35:21 NIV

When our hearts are moved, we should not ignore them. A pull at the heart is grounded in God's invitation. When our willingness is paired with conviction, nothing can stop us from doing what we feel called to.

When it was time to build the tabernacle, it was a group effort. It required the strength and various skills of all who would jump in and lend a hand. Their work was a part of their offering to the Lord. What group efforts are needed to create spaces where God is glorified today? Let's pay attention to the pull of our hearts and put our willingness to work into action.

God, you are worthy of my sacrifice and my time. Your love is worth paying attention to as it moves my heart toward what you want to do in this world. Use me, Lord.

Scripture Reading: Exodus 38-40

Obedience Pays Off

The people of Israel followed all of the LORD's instructions to Moses. Then Moses inspected all their work. When he found it had been done just as the LORD had commanded him, he blessed them.

EXODUS 39:42-43 NLT

There is blessing when we follow the instruction of the Lord. It isn't blind obedience to honor the Lord. When we refuse to take shortcuts and do the work with diligence, the payoff is palpable.

Let's honor the Lord by doing what we know to do. Instead of looking for ways around the hard work, let's partner with God and ask for guidance when we need it. We don't have to pretend to know more than we do. We don't have to know every step to get started.

God, I don't want to hesitate in what you have shown me to do any longer. Give me vision and strength to follow through. I know you will bless me as I follow you.

Scripture Reading: Leviticus 1-3

Peace Offering

"If his offering is a sacrifice of peace offering, if he offers an animal from the herd, male or female, he shall offer it without blemish before the LORD."

LEVITICUS 3:1 ESV

A peace offering is a powerful representation of how we can be united with God. God doesn't want only what we can offer him. He doesn't need our work, though he blesses it. He wants our fellowship.

Friendship with God is available today. Peace with God is present. Jesus' sacrifice was the final offering needed to bring us eternal peace with the Father. He was the pure sacrificial Lamb that took away the sins of the world. There is nothing standing between us and God but Christ, and he welcomes us with open arms. He rains redemption over our surrendered hearts and brings us into the confident rest of his peace.

Savior, thank you for paying the ultimate price that I might have uninterrupted peace with God.

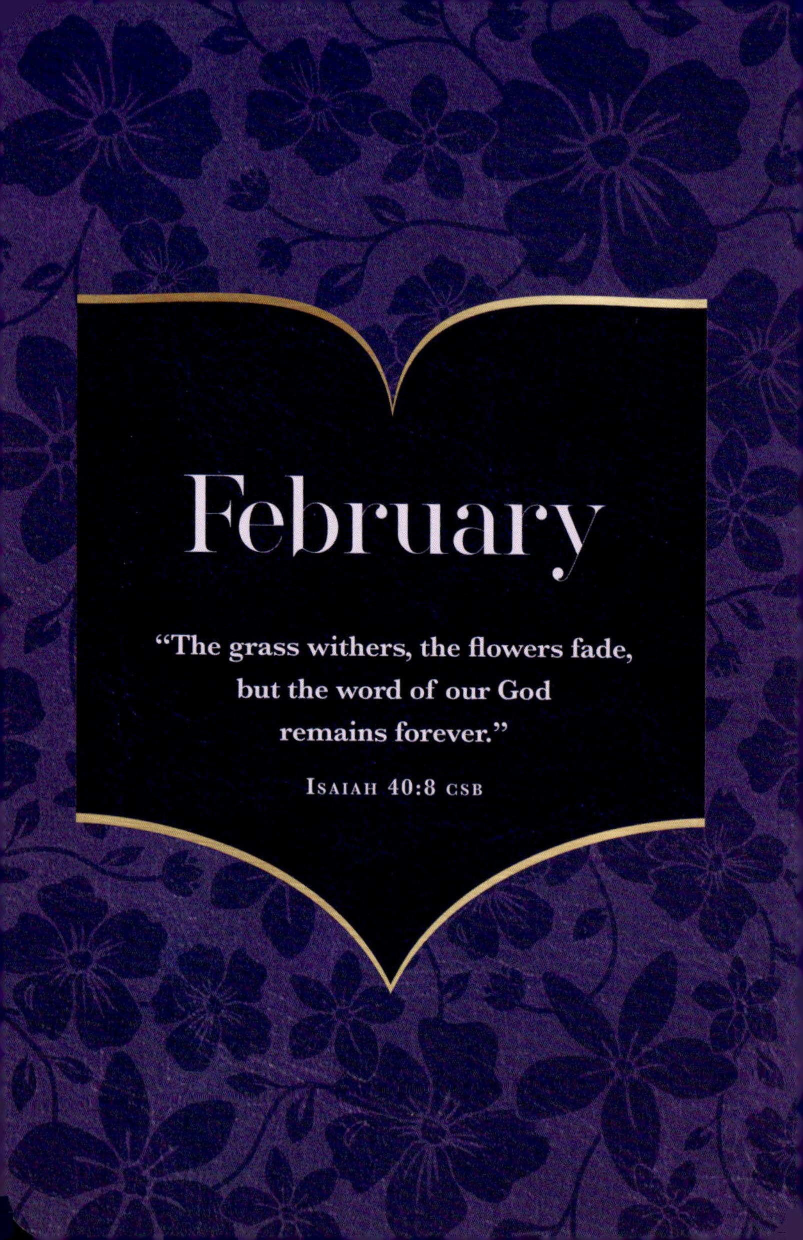

February

"The grass withers, the flowers fade,
but the word of our God
remains forever."

Isaiah 40:8 csb

Scripture Reading: Leviticus 4-6

Needed Repair

Once he has sinned and acknowledged his guilt—he must return what he stole or defrauded… or anything else about which he swore falsely. He will make full restitution for it and add a fifth of its value to it. He is to pay it to its owner on the day he acknowledges his guilt.

LEVITICUS 6:4-5 CSB

Forgiveness is wonderful. God has so much mercy on us, and he readily forgives the repentant heart. Repentance isn't just about easing our guilt in the moment though. It requires turning from our old ways and choosing new ones.

God's Word includes restoration as an act of repentance. We are sometimes too quick to move on from our mistakes and sin. Repairing trust is not easy. It doesn't feel good to admit our wrongdoing. But it is a powerful act of humble repentance to return and restore what was lost.

Lord, help me to take courage when I have seen the error of my ways, not only to choose a different path, but also to make restitution where possible.

Scripture Reading: Leviticus 7-9

Power and Glory

When they came out and blessed the people, the glory of the LORD appeared to all the people. Then fire went out from the LORD and consumed the burnt offering and the portions of fat on the altar; and when all the people saw it, they shouted and fell face downward.

LEVITICUS 9:22-24 NASB

The glory of God is beautiful, but it is also powerful. It is like a fire that falls, consuming our meager offerings. When we surrender our hearts to the Lord, we will witness his power in the inner transformation.

What we lay on the altar before the Lord, he consumes. The sin that we could not shake is overcome by his presence. He burns it up, removing the guilt of our sins. He does what we could never do on our own, and he makes us new. What a powerful reason to worship him today!

Glorious God, there is no one like you. You remove the stain of my wrongs with the power of your glorious love that falls like fire on my surrendered heart. I worship you.

Scripture Reading: Leviticus 10-12

Discernment

That you may distinguish between holy and unholy, and between unclean and clean, and that you may teach the children of Israel all the statutes which the Lord has spoken to them by the hand of Moses.

Leviticus 10:10-11 NKJV

The priests in the tabernacle were instructed to remain clear-headed as they entered the temple. It was their responsibility to teach the law of the Lord to the people, and this required both wisdom and discernment.

If you want to be able to distinguish between holy and unholy, it is not enough to know the Word of God. You must also remain open and discerning. This is not to say you will perfectly live it out. But when you go to into the tabernacle of meeting, when you are teaching others about the ways of the Lord, it is important to be free from influences that cloud your understanding.

Lord, you are the wise one. I want to grow in discernment, and I know that means being intentional about the influences I let into my life. Show me where I can make more room for you today.

Scripture Reading: Leviticus 13-15

Healing as a Process

"When a person who discharges a body fluid is made clean, he must count seven days for himself for his cleansing. He must wash his clothes and bathe his body in fresh water, and he will be clean."

Leviticus 15:13 NCV

When we ask the Lord to heal us, he does not do it the same way each time. Some healing happens instantly, but much of the healing we experience in life is a process. It can be tempting to feel discouraged when it doesn't happen how we want, but it does not mean the Lord isn't at work.

Some things take time. We can see this throughout Scripture. Let's not rush the process or abandon our faith in God by declaring ourselves exceptions to his merciful care. He is with us, and he shows us what is needed. We do what we can and trust him with the rest.

Healer, thank you for the power of your love that rights what is wrong. Where I have been impatient, show me the steps to take and be with me in the waiting.

Scripture Reading: Leviticus 16-18

Words to Live By

"Keep my decrees and laws, for the person who obeys them will live by them. I am the LORD."

LEVITICUS 18:5 NIV

Obedience to the Lord isn't just what is required; it is good for us. He knows what we need before we even realize its necessity. His perspective is full in every age, and he knows what he is doing. If he asks us to follow him, it is not without reason.

When we choose to follow Christ's example, he helps us stay on the path of God's loving guidance. The heart of God's law is for our salvation and freedom, and we find that fully in Christ. He fulfilled the requirements of the law so that we are free to walk in his ways with confidence and trust.

Lord Jesus, you are the source of life. Lead me in your ways and guide me as I follow you. My ears are open. Speak to me.

Scripture Reading: Leviticus 19-21

Love Your Neighbor

"Do not seek revenge or bear a grudge against a fellow Israelite, but love your neighbor as yourself. I am the LORD."

LEVITICUS 19:18 NLT

Jesus famously quoted this verse when questioned about the most important part of the Law of Moses (Matthew 22:36-40). First, we are to love the Lord wholeheartedly, with our entire souls and minds. Out of this love we are to also love our neighbors as we love ourselves.

But the lesson doesn't stop there. In Luke 10:29, a religious scholar asked, "Who is my neighbor?" In response, Jesus told the parable of the Good Samaritan. A true neighbor is the one who shows mercy and helps when there is a need. Let's love our neighbors well, letting God's mercy move us, and stop getting caught up in details that distract us from action.

Merciful One, thank you for the reminder that loving my neighbor has less to do with who they are and more to do with who I am in you. Let me be a living example of your love.

Scripture Reading: Leviticus 22-24

Sacred Rest

"Six days shall work be done, but on the seventh day is a Sabbath of solemn rest, a holy convocation. You shall do no work. It is a Sabbath to the LORD in all your dwelling places."

LEVITICUS 23:3 ESV

Rest is a rhythm of creation. God took time to rest and enjoy what he made, and we are to do the same. Our bodies, minds, and hearts need restorative time. In this busy world, we have many excuses to keep moving, keep checking things off the list, and to put rest off for another day. We need a reclamation of scheduled rest!

Instead of pushing until we break, let's take the lead from the Lord himself and institute a day of Sabbath. Rest isn't only sitting around. We need restful connection with others, creative outputs, and nature adventures.

Lord, I want to be intentional with rest and not just wait for a good time to do it. I know you made me to need breaks, so I follow your design and choose to rest.

Scripture Reading: Leviticus 25-27

Ten Percent

"Every tenth of the land's produce, grain from the soil or fruit from the trees, belongs to the LORD; it is holy to the LORD."

LEVITICUS 27:30 CSB

What if we really took tithing seriously and went beyond our finances? If we offered ten percent of our time back to the Lord, what would that look like? In a week (taking out eight hours for sleep), that looks like an hour and a half each day. That might feel overwhelming, but what if it didn't have to all be spent in church, devotions, or prayer?

If we live in open-hearted surrender, an hour and a half a day could encompass Christ-centered conversations, walking in nature and keeping a curious eye open for God's fingerprints around us, or volunteering to help a neighbor. God honors our offerings. Let's offer him ten percent of our resources including our time.

Creator, you are worthy of my attention, my surrender, and my devotion. Give me eyes and inspiration to see how I can offer you more of my time.

Scripture Reading: Numbers 1-3

Set Apart

"Bring the tribe of Levi forward and present them before Aaron the priest, that they may serve him. They shall perform the duties for him and for the whole congregation in front of the tent of meeting, to do the service of the tabernacle."

NUMBERS 3:6-7 NASB

The tribe of Levi was set apart to serve the Lord and the people as priests. It was their sacred work to be consecrated in this way. Some are following that priestly calling today, and those who do rely on the Lord's provision through his people.

Being consecrated for the Lord is wonderful, and it can look different for everyone. Jesus was set apart, and he spent his ministry traveling, teaching, and healing. Before this time in his life, he worked in carpentry. Nothing is wasted in God's kingdom. He uses everything to prepare us for following his lead.

Lord, thank you for meeting me in my work. Even the most natural work becomes sacred when you are in it.

Scripture Reading: Numbers 4-6

Priestly Blessing

"The LORD bless you and keep you;
The LORD make His face shine upon you,
And be gracious to you;
The LORD lift up His countenance upon you,
And give you peace."
NUMBERS 6:24-26 NKJV

Receive this priestly blessing today as you reread the Scripture. It is not only meant for those who came before. It is an active blessing we can pray every day. There is blessing, care, and kindness in the presence of your heavenly Father. There is grace among the beauty of his watchful eye. There is peace to settle your heart, mind, and body.

Jesus is the Prince of Peace. Lean into his loving arms as you settle into this moment. Spend some time in prayer before moving quickly on and ask the Lord to calm you with the power of his peaceful presence. He is near, and he makes his face shine upon you!

Lord, thank you for your goodness, faithfulness, and peace.

Scripture Reading: Numbers 7-9

At His Command

Sometimes the cloud stayed over the Tent for a long time, but the Israelites obeyed the LORD and did not move. Sometimes the cloud was over it only a few days. At the LORD's command the people camped, and at his command they moved.

NUMBERS 9:19-20 NCV

The Lord's command was connected to his presence. When he moved, his people moved. When he stayed, they stayed. When we are connected to the Holy Spirit through relationship with Jesus Christ, we have the presence of the living God with us. We don't have to guess what he would have us do. He has given us the Living Word in Christ, and he leads us with his wisdom.

How cognizant are you of where God wants you to be? Do you sense his cloud hovering? Or do you sense him shifting and leading you into something new? He will never leave you or forsake you. Follow him, and you will be satisfied.

Spirit, lead me and give me patience when you want me to stay where I am.

Scripture Reading: Numbers 10-12

Shift in Perspective

"If only we had meat to eat! We remember the fish we ate in Egypt at no cost—also the cucumbers, melons, leeks, onions and garlic. But now we have lost our appetite; we never see anything but this manna!"

NUMBERS 11:4-6 NIV

It's easy to judge the Israelites with the benefit of hindsight, but we are as human and prone to wander as they were. How often do we experience the kindness of God's provision and complain that it isn't more? We grow tired of what we know and compare what we have to what we could have. All the while, we leave out the negative aspects we left behind.

What we need is a perspective shift. God's gracious hand supplies what we need. Is there bread enough today? Do we have what we need? A place to lay our heads at night, food on the table, and clean water to drink? Let's give thanks for the provision in the moment. Instead of complaining, we can turn our requests to God with grateful hearts.

Lord, help me to have a heart of cultivated gratitude as I trust you for more.

Scripture Reading: Numbers 13-15

Bold Faith

Caleb tried to quiet the people as they stood before Moses. "Let's go at once to take the land," he said. "We can certainly conquer it!"

NUMBERS 13:30 NLT

When Caleb returned from the scouting trip to see the land that the Lord promised his people, he had a strong conviction that it was already theirs. He didn't see the people of the land as a threat because he trusted that what the Lord said he would faithfully do. He was in the very small percentage that felt this way.

The worries of the others caused the people to fear. They even went so far as to want to stone Joshua and Caleb! Their bold faith was unwavering. When you come up against a challenge and have the confident promise of God, don't give into the worried fears of others. Let the Lord's promise be your foundation, and stand on it with bold faith.

Faithful One, I want the faith of Caleb that saw the promised land through eyes of faith. Help me to walk boldly.

Scripture Reading: Numbers 16-18

Inheritance

"To the Levites I have given every tithe in Israel for an inheritance, in return for their service that they do, their service in the tent of meeting,"

NUMBERS 18:21 ESV

If you don't have an earthly inheritance, don't fear. Money and resources come and go, but the faithful provision of the Lord is unwavering. If you follow the Lord and trust his provision, you can take heart that he is your inheritance, and he will continue to provide for you.

It is wise to store up what we can for a rainy day, but it is unwise to hoard our resources out of a scarcity mindset. The Lord is generous, and he calls us to be generous as we partner with his heart. While we offer him our hearts, our lives, and our trust, we follow in his footsteps, relying on his provision and opening our stockpiles to share with those in need.

Provider, you are my great inheritance. I know I can trust you to provide even when I don't know how it will come. Lead me in generosity.

Scripture Reading: Numbers 19-21

The Heart of It

"Take the staff and assemble the community. You and your brother Aaron are to speak to the rock while they watch, and it will yield its water. You will bring out water for them from the rock and provide drink for the community and their livestock."

NUMBERS 20:7-8 CSB

Reading this passage, there is a distinct difference in what the Lord instructed Moses and Aaron to do, and how they followed through with it. In verses ten and eleven, Moses gathered the people and scolded them. He yelled at them and hit the rock with the staff, and water came gushing out.

The resulting water happened, but Moses did not act in the spirit of God's heart. How often do we do the same? We follow through on the Lord's command, but we want everyone to know it isn't because we want to. There are consequences when we act in obedience without love. Let's make sure God's heart penetrates our own before we do what we are called to do.

Lord, I want to remain humble before you, so you can demonstrate your powerful holiness through me.

Scripture Reading: Numbers 22-24

Promise Keeper

God is not a man, that He would lie,
Nor a son of man, that He would change His mind;
Has He said, and will He not do it?
Or has He spoken, and will He not make it good?
NUMBERS 23:19 NASB

God is not only faithful to the vows he makes with others. He is faithful to follow through on everything he has said. God is full of truth. There is no shadow in him. He does not manipulate or embellish. He is capable of doing all he has said he will do. We only have to trust him.

Depending on the kinds of people we are used to dealing with, our expectations of follow-through may vary. There is one who is unwavering in truth. God does not lie. He is unable to be swayed by power, influence, or resources. He stands firm in truth, and he always will.

God, you are incorruptible. You are full of truth and wisdom, and you never go back on your promises or act against your nature. Thank you!

Scripture Reading: Numbers 25-27

Eyes to See

"Go up into this Mount Abarim, and see the land which I have given to the children of Israel."

NUMBERS 27:12 NKJV

Even though Moses could not enter the Promised Land with the new generation, God allowed him to see it. Up on a mountain, he caught a glimpse of Israel's future. He saw it for what it was: the Lord's faithfulness to the following generations.

If you will follow the Lord and yield to his leadership, God will bring you to a higher perspective to see what's coming. He may just give you a glimpse of the fulfillment of his promise for future generations even if you won't experience yourself. In restorative mercy, God offers his devoted lovers the ability to taste and see that he is good.

Lord, encourage my heart in hope and give me eyes to see what you have in store for those who follow in your footsteps.

Scripture Reading: Numbers 28-30

Daily Connection

"Give this command to the Israelites. Tell them: 'Bring me food offerings made by fire, for a smell that is pleasing to me, and be sure to bring them at the right time.'"

NUMBERS 28:1-2 NCV

The right time today's verse speaks of is within the context of daily offerings. God wants, and has always wanted, consistent connection with his people. He wants us to know him as much as he wants to know us. His desire is that we would come to him daily and find our sustenance and strength in his presence.

When we make devotional living a daily practice, where we offer God our attention, our time, and our surrendered love, he delights over us and fills us with his presence.

Lord, I hunger and thirst for righteousness. More than that, I hunger and thirst for you! I bring you my surrendered heart today as an offering.

Scripture Reading: Numbers 31-33

Praise and Thanks

"Your servants have counted the soldiers under our command, and not one is missing. So we have brought as an offering… to make atonement for ourselves before the LORD."

NUMBERS 31:49-50 NIV

Not one soldier was unaccounted for or lost to the battlefield on this day. God's people experienced the powerful protection of the Lord. What was their response? It is the same we can offer him today. The rightful response to God's mercy is worship.

When God moves in your life, don't simply move on. Let it lead you to him in gratitude. Thank him for what he's done, and worship him for his powerful care of you. Every act of mercy, every fulfillment of love is an expression of his unwavering faithfulness toward you.

Father, you are more than a wise leader, you are my defender and protector. I worship you for how you are already moving on my behalf.

Scripture Reading: Numbers 34-36

Cities of Refuge

"Six of the towns you give the Levites will be cities of refuge"
NUMBERS 35:6 NLT

God planned places of refuge for people so they could experience respite from their troubles. These were safe spaces where those who had done wrong could seek refuge and due process. They were places the accused could go and be protected from retribution. Instead of taking vengeance (God says vengeance is his), let's allow for places of refuge where we can also experience the patience of mercy and justice.

God's presence is our greatest refuge. The cities of refuge served to foreshadow the salvation and peace we find in Christ. He is the place we run and find true justice, redemption, and safety for our souls.

Redeemer, you always made provisions for those who were on the outside and needed a safe space to run. You have become that safe space, and I come to find rest in your presence today.

Scripture Reading: Deuteronomy 1-3

Great God

O LORD God, you have only begun to show your servant your greatness and your mighty hand. For what god is there in heaven or on earth who can do such works and mighty acts as yours?

DEUTERONOMY 3:24 ESV

God went before his people, fought for them, led them, and delivered them. He does the same for you! The greatness of God is unmatched, and it isn't only the power that created this world. Mercy is at the center of all he does. No one can do what he has done, and no one can undo it. His love is as strong today as it ever has been or ever will be.

You have only begun to witness God's greatness and mighty hand. He is always at work, always moving in mercy and following through in faithfulness. What he has begun, he will continue.

Great God, there is no one else like you in all the world, and I have only caught the smallest glimpses of your power. Reveal yourself to me as I continue to look to you.

Scripture Reading: Deuteronomy 4-6

Wholehearted Love

"Love the LORD your God with all your heart, with all your soul, and with all your strength."

DEUTERONOMY 6:5 CSB

The greatest commandment is to love the Lord your God with all your heart, soul, and strength. This hasn't changed! Jesus confirmed the power of this truth in Matthew 22:37. It remains the first and greatest commandment.

If you do nothing else to grow in your relationship with the Lord today, may it be in this foundational thing. First Corinthians thirteen is a good place to begin to understand how you can implement practical love in your life. What would it look like for you to love God with all your heart? How about your mind? What kind of strength could you offer to put it toward loving the Lord?

God, I want to love you as more than an idea or profession of faith. I want to love you in detailed action and humble surrender. Show me the way to love you well.

Scripture Reading: Deuteronomy 7-9

Faithful through Generations

"Know therefore that the LORD your God, He is God, the faithful God, who keeps His covenant and His faithfulness to a thousand generations for those who love Him and keep His commandments."

DEUTERONOMY 7:9 NASB

God's faithfulness is amazing. He keeps his Word not only to those he made the vow with, but to subsequent generations. If you ever wonder whether you're included under the umbrella of God's faithfulness, you can rest assured, you aren't too late. You are right on time.

The Lord hasn't stopped weaving the details of our lives together in redemptive mercy since he first promised salvation. In Christ, we are living in the fullness of his promise. He is still working the rest together in his perfect time. He will continue to be faithful throughout the generations.

Faithful One, I trust that you are still doing what you set out to do. I trust your nature, and I rest in you.

Scripture Reading: Deuteronomy 10-12

Defender

"He administers justice for the fatherless and the widow, and loves the stranger, giving him food and clothing. Therefore love the stranger, for you were strangers in the land of Egypt."

DEUTERONOMY 10:18-19 NKJV

As God takes care of the vulnerable, so should we. It matters how we treat those who may feel on the outside of things. Jesus broke down the invisible walls of hostility that people put up in the name of God and showed the true nature of his kindness: openhearted welcome and justice for the oppressed.

It is difficult to love the stranger. It also isn't optional. It is important to remember that we have all been on the outside at one time, and God welcomed us into his family with open arms. Let's show his same generosity by extending the kindness we find in him to others.

Lord, when I would rather sit by and not come to the defense of those who need it, remind me who you are. I want to partner with your purposes.

Scripture Reading: Deuteronomy 13-15

Loyal to the Lord

"Serve only the Lord your God. Respect him, keep his commands, and obey him. Serve him and be loyal to him."

Deuteronomy 13:4 NCV

There are many things vying for our attention these days. This isn't a new phenomena. There have always been false prophets who claim to speak in the name of the Lord but aren't anything like him. More than teachers, more than confident and powerful people, we are to be loyal to the Lord.

God's nature has been revealed through Jesus Christ. We don't have to wonder what he is like. He is merciful. He is true. He is powerful. He is just. There is no need for control. He is gentle. He is kind. He is a servant to all. He is our Savior, and in him we find the way, the truth, and the life. Give him your loyalty.

Jesus Christ, I choose to follow your ways, even when others distort your character and your Word. You have my loyalty, for you are always good.

Scripture Reading: Deuteronomy 16-18

As You Are Able

"Each of you must bring a gift in proportion to the way the LORD your God has blessed you."
DEUTERONOMY 16:17 NIV

Fair is not the same thing as equitable. God's example for us is not to give the same amount. A tithe is a percentage because the amount changes depending on what we have. When we bring our gift to the Lord, let's not compare it with our neighbor's. Let's pay no attention to what others offer. Our measure is dependent on what we have!

The widow's mite (Luke 21:1-4) was an incredible sacrifice. She gave more than the rest because she gave out of what she didn't have. The Lord honors our offerings in a very personal way. Let's keep this in mind when we bring our gifts before him.

Lord, I'm so glad you are a personal God. You know me better than anyone else. I don't have to prove a thing. Be honored by the gift I offer you today.

Scripture Reading: Deuteronomy 19-21

Influences

"Then the officers will also say, 'Is anyone here afraid or worried? If you are, you may go home before you frighten anyone else.'"

DEUTERONOMY 20:8 NLT

Before going to war, there were regulations to send some of the men home. It wasn't as punishment but for protection! Among the many reasons the men could return home, there was one that stands out as protection, not for the men leaving, but for the men who would stay to fight.

When we are going into a situation where we need bold courage and faith, it matters what voices we listen to. If some are prone to being preoccupied by fear or worry, we should create boundaries. When we need encouragement, it is people who believe that we can handle what we face with God on our side that we should keep close.

Lord, help me to remember that the company I keep matters. The influences I listen to may eventually sway me, so I thank you for discernment.

Scripture Reading: Deuteronomy 22-24

Curses into Blessings

"The LORD your God would not listen to Balaam; instead the LORD your God turned the curse into a blessing for you, because the LORD your God loved you."

DEUTERONOMY 23:5 ESV

God does not let the curses of others influence his faithfulness. He is loyal in love, and he turns what was meant as a curse into a blessing. Genesis 50:20 echoes this thought, "you meant evil against me, but God meant it for good, to bring it about that many people should be kept alive." Remember Joseph's life? He was cursed by his brothers, but it turned into a blessing for all of them!

This is how powerful God is. He can take even the bitterness of our own hearts and bring blessing through the way he weaves his redemptive love through the details of our lives. There is hope for us all! No matter what we have done or experienced, there is blessing awaiting us.

Lord, thank you for the power of your redemptive mercy that makes even what was meant for harm a place of breakthrough. I praise you!

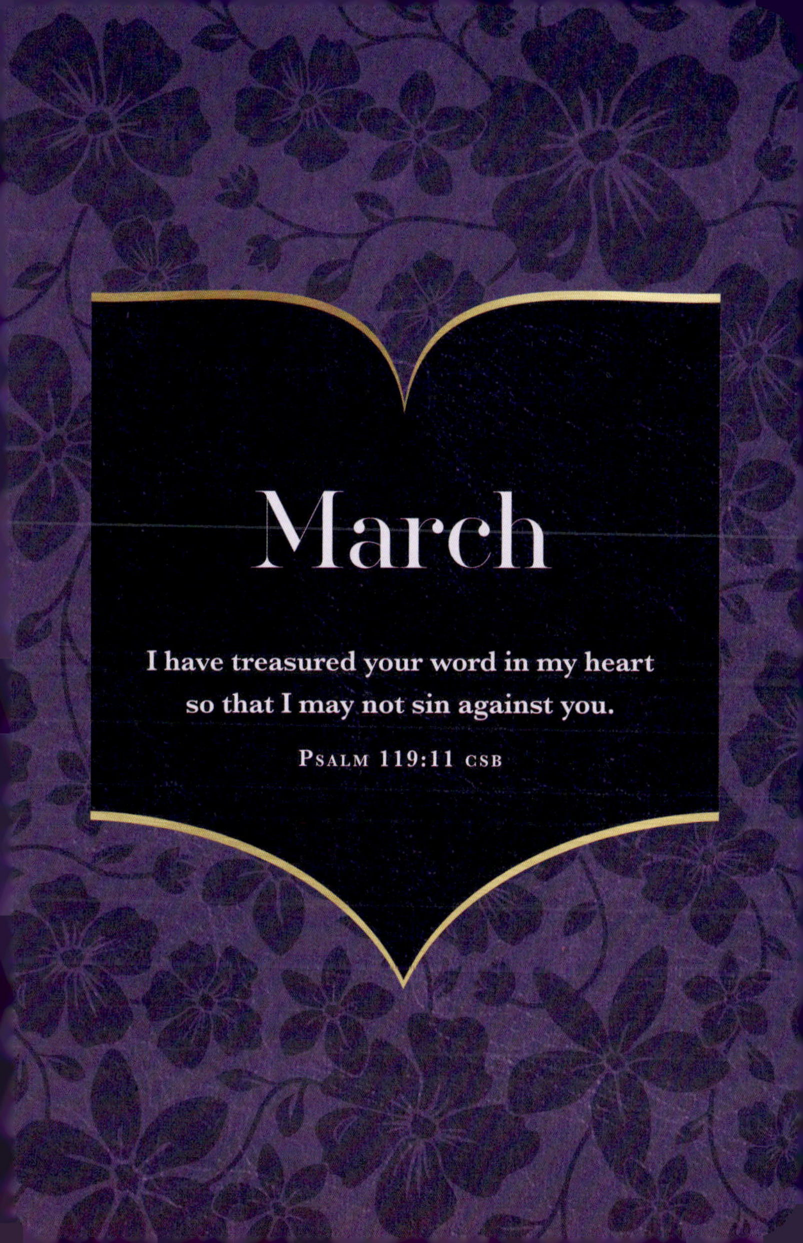

March

I have treasured your word in my heart
so that I may not sin against you.

Psalm 119:11 csb

Scripture Reading: Deuteronomy 25-27

Integrity Matters

"Do not have differing weights in your bag, one heavy and one light… You must have a full and honest weight, a full and honest dry measure, so that you may live long in the land the LORD your God is giving you."

DEUTERONOMY 25:13-15 CSB

Unfair measures don't honor people, and they don't honor God. When the Word instructs us to love the Lord our God with all our hearts, souls, and minds, and to love our neighbors as ourselves, that includes how we live and conduct our business.

Love is not something that changes depending on whom we're dealing with. The standard of love remains the same, though our willingness to choose it may vary with those we are around. Truth, honesty, and trust are foundational to God's kingdom.

Lord, I want to walk in your ways in Spirit and in truth. May my life be filled with your humble love, your powerful justice, and your persistent peace.

Scripture Reading: Deuteronomy 28-30

Blessed in Every Way

"Blessed will you be in the city, and blessed will you be in the country. Blessed will be your basket and your kneading bowl. Blessed will you be when you come in, and blessed will you be when you go out."

DEUTERONOMY 28:3,5-6 NASB

Blessing doesn't happen by accident. As we read the Word, we see that obedient devotion leads to blessing. Deuteronomy 28:2 assures, "All these blessings will come to you if you obey the Lord your God."

A blessed life is one that is rooted in humble devotion to the Lord. When we humble ourselves before God and follow in his ways, he leads us beside still waters. He gives restoration, grace, and peace. We cannot control how others receive or perceive us, but we can follow the Lord and trust his heart to keep us close and deliver us into pastures of peace at the right time.

Lord, I know obedience to your law leads to blessing. I choose to follow you in word and deed.

Scripture Reading: Deuteronomy 31-34

Stand in Courage

"Be strong and of good courage, do not fear nor be afraid of them; for the LORD your God, He is the One who goes with you. He will not leave you nor forsake you."

DEUTERONOMY 31:6 NKJV

The promise of God's presence is repeated throughout Scripture. Promise of a peaceful life without any trouble? Not so much. We have the promised peace of God as our portion, but that doesn't mean it won't be tested. The Bible quotes God as saying "Do not be afraid" three hundred sixty-five times. Every day, we have a reminder to stand in courage because God's faithfulness is our foundation.

When we feel fear setting in, let's not allow it to convince us we're doing something wrong. Courage comes when we feel the fear and continue to do what we know to do. We can trust God to go with us into every situation.

Lord, you are my courage. Thank you for your presence and your peace that permeates my heart and mind as I set my attention on you.

Scripture Reading: Joshua 1-3

Blessed Assurance

"No one will be able to defeat you all your life. Just as I was with Moses, so I will be with you. I will not leave you or forget you."

JOSHUA 1:5 NCV

The book of Joshua begins with an assurance from God. Just as he was with Moses, he promised to be with Joshua. This was no small thing! Joshua was tasked with leading God's people into the Promised Land. It would require trust, confidence in God, and strength to move ahead.

Before you enter a new season, you might feel excitement and then fear of what it might require. You don't have to be afraid! God will go with you as you look to him. His presence will be close as you walk in his ways. Don't let fear keep you from moving ahead. God's call on your life is backed up by his presence and power. Let fellowship with your God be your confidence.

Lord, I need reassurance from your presence that I am not alone today. Thank you for your faithfulness to your people and to me.

Scripture Reading: Joshua 4-6

Powerful Results

When the trumpets sounded, the army shouted, and at the sound of the trumpet, when the men gave a loud shout, the wall collapsed.

JOSHUA 6:20 NIV

Obedience leads to the powerful promises of God. They are not a theory. They will come to pass, just as he said they would. God instructed his people to march around the walls of the city of Jericho seven times. This wasn't a formula. They had never done it before. They had to trust and obey.

Obedience requires trust. God rarely moves in the same way in our lives because he wants us to rely on his presence—not a formula. Relationship is what allows us to experience the faithfulness of God as we take him at his Word. Will you trust God to miraculously move when you follow his wisdom?

Lord, I don't want to question your ways. When I can't understand why you ask me to do something, help me to follow your lead and trust you.

Scripture Reading: Joshua 7-9

God's Counsel

The Israelites examined their food,
but they did not consult the LORD.
JOSHUA 9:14 NLT

Consulting with the Lord throughout our day matters. He has wisdom to guide us if only we seek out his perspective and listen! He knows the way through, around, and behind. The God who sees all is the God who loves to direct us when we ask for guidance.

When we go about making our own choices, God doesn't abandon us. He is with us in them. But he has a fuller picture to share if we make time for him. We could save ourselves some trouble by including the Lord in our decision-making process.

Lord, I so often just do my own thing and then consult you later. I know you never leave me, even when I find myself in messes of my own making. I'm grateful for your mercy!

Scripture Reading: Joshua 10-12

Peace to Rest

Joshua took the whole land, according to all that the LORD had spoken to Moses. And Joshua gave it for an inheritance to Israel according to their tribal allotments. And the land had rest from war.

JOSHUA 11:23 ESV

The book of Joshua is filled with tales of the battles Israel fought as they followed God. They trusted the Lord to guide them and fight for them. They trusted him to tear down walls and dry up river beds. When they entered the Promised Land, their inheritance was sure.

Peace was a product of this fulfillment, though it did not last forever. In this world, there are many battles. There is ongoing conflict, but let's not take for granted the pockets of peace we also experience. There is peace in Christ, and it is always available in the fellowship of his Spirit. Go to him, your promised peace, and find rest today.

God of Peace, you are the one who gives me space to rest. You are my refuge. May I find your perfect peace here in this moment, no matter what came before or what comes next.

Scripture Reading: Joshua 13-15

Faith-filled Boldness

Hebron still belongs to Caleb son of Jephunneh the Kenizzite as an inheritance today because he followed the LORD, the God of Israel, completely.

JOSHUA 14:14 CSB

If you have ever wondered whether your faith-filled convictions matter, be encouraged. Caleb and Joshua were the only ones from their generation allowed to enter the Promised Land. This was because they believed God's Word over the fear of what they faced. They trusted that the one who called them would faithfully do all that he promised. He did, and they got to taste the fruit!

Caleb's reward for living a life of faith-filled boldness was a lasting inheritance. God always honors those who honor him. There is a beautiful reward for faith, although by no means does it earn our salvation.

Lord, I don't want to let the fear of what feels obvious keep me from faith in what you can do miraculously. May my heart grow in courage as I follow you.

Scripture Reading: Joshua 16-18

Active Faith

Joshua said to them, "If you are a numerous people, go up to the forest and clear a place for yourself there in the land of the Perizzites and of the Rephaim, since the hill country of Ephraim is too narrow for you."

JOSHUA 17:15 NASB

Faith requires belief and trust, but it also requires action at the right time. When God gives us direction, let's not just add it to the wisdom we're weighing. Let's follow through and act on it! Faith and obedience go hand in hand.

When you have the next step to take, don't wait any longer. When there is clear action to take, partner your faith with follow-through. God loves to lead. When we outgrow where we've been, it means there is something greater for us to enter into. Look to God and follow his leadership.

Father, thank you for your goodness and faithfulness. I am sometimes hesitant to change, but I trust what you are leading me into is full of goodness.

Scripture Reading: Joshua 19-21

Unfailing

Not a word failed of any good thing which the LORD had spoken to the house of Israel. All came to pass.
JOSHUA 21:45 NKJV

Every promise of God is a "yes and amen," as 2 Corinthians 1:20 says. Christ is the fulfillment of every longing, but that does not mean God loses sight of the details. If you ask the Spirit to reveal where God's hand of faithfulness has been upon your life, you will be surprised to see how thorough, thoughtful, and persistent his mercy is.

God remains unfailing in faithfulness today. He is still working out his promises, and you can trust him to do it. While you are waiting with patience in one area, don't forget to look for God's goodness in another. Praise will flow as you build a garden of gratitude in your heart for all he has done.

Faithful Lord, you always do what you say you will. Fill my heart, mind, and body with your peace as I trust you.

Scripture Reading: Joshua 22-24

Our Wellspring

"Be careful to obey the teachings and laws Moses, the LORD's servant, gave you: to love the LORD your God and obey his commands, to continue to follow him and serve him the very best you can."

JOSHUA 22:5 NCV

We might feel our need for God more in times of pressure, but God's faithful nature never changes. In times of both feast and famine, God is our source. He is our wellspring of life! In his presence, we are restored, renewed, and released.

Let's keep first things first and come before the Lord each day with open hearts and willing hands. As we love the Lord in word and in action, this is our offering. We follow his lead and serve him the very best we can. He expects nothing more. Let's resist the need to do things perfectly and instead do things connectedly!

My Source, to know you is to love you, and to love you is to follow you. I put you first today. I welcome your leadership over my mind, heart, and actions.

Scripture Reading: Judges 1-3

God-given Help

The LORD raised up judges, who saved them out of the hands of these raiders.

JUDGES 2:16 NIV

You've probably noticed the cycles of humanity in reading the Bible up to this point. God's people honored the Lord, and they experienced his blessing. Then they went their own way and left God out of it. After some time, they experienced the consequences of their actions. As they humbled themselves, God restored them. Before we judge those who came before, let's be aware of our own patterns.

God is great at giving second (and five hundredth) chances. He readily restores the repentant heart. He provides help when his people need it. Wherever you find yourself today, no matter what circumstance, God is close and ready to help you.

God, thank you for your restoration when I turn in repentance. I don't want to depend on my own strength, for I will surely fail. You are my God, and I will follow you.

Scripture Reading: Judges 4-6

Get Ready

Deborah said to Barak, "Get ready! This is the day the LORD will give you victory over Sisera, for the LORD is marching ahead of you." So Barak led his 10,000 warriors down the slopes of Mount Tabor into battle.

JUDGES 4:14 NLT

Deborah gave the message of the Lord to Barak, but he wanted more assurance. He said he would go ahead if Deborah would accompany them (verse eight). God did end up giving them victory that day, but the honor went to a brave woman, Jael.

God doesn't discriminate. He has been using women from the beginning. Look at Ruth, Rahab, Esther, Deborah, and Jael. They were powerful displays of strong faith, and their courage was honored. Take courage, for the Lord will honor you as you honor him!

Creator, I know you don't make mistakes, and that includes when you created me. I am as valuable to you as any other, and I'm so grateful to know your love. I partner with you and your ways. Use me for the glory of your name.

Scripture Reading: Judges 7-9

Small but Mighty

"You are too many for me to give the Midianites into their hand, lest Israel boast over me, saying, 'My own hand has saved me.' With the 300 men who lapped I will save you and give the Midianites into your hand, and let all the others go every man to his home."

JUDGES 7:2,7 ESV

God reveals his power through our weakness. In the case of today's verse, that meant sending the majority of the Israelite army home. God doesn't need big numbers to move. His glory shines the brightest when we cannot rely on logic. His miraculous mercy is on display when the odds are stacked against us.

When you find yourself in lean times, don't be discouraged. Sometimes God may even encourage you to do less and rely on him more. He will do what no one else can and deliver you in ways you couldn't have anticipated. Though you are small, God is still mighty.

Lord, you are the miracle maker, and your power shines through in magnificent ways. I trust you when the odds feel impossible. You are for me.

Scripture Reading: Judges 10-12

Spirit Empowerment

The Spirit of the LORD came on Jephthah, who traveled through Gilead and Manasseh, and then through Mizpah of Gilead. He crossed over to the Ammonites from Mizpah of Gilead.

JUDGES 11:29 CSB

Jephthah was a great warrior, but he was an outcast. As an illegitimate son of Gilead, he was run off his family's land and ridiculed. By now, we see that God doesn't care where we come from. He didn't label Jephthah as unworthy. He honored him as one who faithfully served him, and eventually others did too.

The past didn't define his identity; the presence of God's Spirit did. When God empowers you, nothing can stop you. If you are in God, he is in you. It doesn't matter what others say about you. Trust the one who called you to honor you. Follow his lead, and you won't be sorry.

Spirit, empower me with your presence and remind me of my identity in you. Drown out the opinions of others and root me in your love.

Scripture Reading: Judges 13-15

Miraculous Hope

Then the angel of the LORD appeared to the woman and said to her, "Behold now, you are infertile and have not given birth; but you will conceive and give birth to a son."

JUDGES 13:3 NASB

God breathes new life into barren areas. He can do what no one else can, and he loves to surprise us with his goodness. Do you have an area of hopelessness? A piece of your life that appears like a barren field? Ask the Lord to breathe on it and speak new life into your heart.

If you earnestly seek the Lord, you will find him. God's Word promises it. Search him out today, and you will be met with the goodness of his presence. He loves to bring new life and miraculous hope into our hearts, homes, and communities.

Lord, do what only you can do and revive my hope. Speak to me, and my soul will be satisfied.

Scripture Reading: Judges 16-18

Another Chance

Then Samson called to the LORD, saying, "O LORD God, remember me, I pray! Strengthen me, I pray, just this once, O God, that I may with one blow take vengeance on the Philistines for my two eyes!"

JUDGES 16:28 NKJV

God responds to the heart that reaches out to him. Though Samson was caught in weakness, he did not let that moment define him. He turned to the Lord and asked for miraculous strength just one more time, knowing it would be the last thing he ever did.

Even when the stakes are not so high, God hears us. He honors those who call out to him. Let's not let our mistakes define us. We may face consequences to our actions; this is natural. But we don't have to carry shame or continue making the same mistakes. We can start fresh right now by asking the Lord to restore our hearts and strengthen us.

Lord God, thank you for the power of your mercy that keeps an attentive ear listening for those who cry to you. Strengthen me today in your grace.

Scripture Reading: Judges 19-21

Rebuild

They went back to the land God had given them and rebuilt their cities and lived there.

Judges 21:23 NCV

Ecclesiastes assures us there is a time for everything including a time to destroy and a time to build. The tribe of Benjamin fought and lost against the rest of Israel, and yet they were still shown mercy. They were not wiped out. They were restored, and they were sent off to rebuild.

Restoration is a beautiful act, but it is not the end. Restoration of relationship is the first step. Next comes the rebuilding phase. When trust has been broken, it's important to recognize that it will take time to rebuild what was lost. Restoration is God's miraculous work, and rebuilding is ours. Let's not forget this important step!

Lord, thank you for the power of restoration and for the responsibility of rebuilding. Help me to reflect your faithful love as I work with others to rebuild what was lost.

Scripture Reading: Ruth 1-4

Devoted Daughter

"Where you go I will go, and where you stay I will stay.
Your people will be my people and your God my God.
Where you die I will die, and there I will be buried."
RUTH 1:16-17 NIV

Ruth wasn't Naomi's daughter by birth, but she was certainly her daughter bonded by love. She wouldn't listen to her mother-in-law's encouragement to go back to her own hometown. Ruth wanted to be with Naomi; she was her chosen mother, and the relationship blessed them both.

God doesn't abandon us in our grief. He doesn't leave us without hope. Even when Naomi felt bitter about her devastating losses, God provided his hope and care. By the end of the book of Ruth, Naomi had reason to rejoice in the birth of a grandson, whose line would become that of King David. God restores what was lost and gives bright new hope!

Lord, where you go I will go, and where you stay I will stay. Thank you for the power of your love in my relationships.

Scripture Reading: 1 Samuel 1-3

Bring God Your Pain

Hannah was in deep anguish, crying bitterly as she prayed to the Lord.

1 Samuel 1:10 NLT

Hannah was in such a fierce state of focused prayer, the priest thought she was drunk. Her heart was in anguish, and she prayed for God to give her a son. Even when others are put off by our deep emotions, God never is. He doesn't keep us at a distance. He draws close in compassion and comfort.

How often do you bring God your pain? You don't have to keep it under wraps, pretending it's not there. And you don't have to dig up anything that isn't there either. He takes you as you are whenever you come to him. Draw near.

Lord, you honored Hannah's prayer, and I ask that you would honor my deep pain as well. Meet me in it, and bring powerful peace, reviving hope, and new life.

Scripture Reading: 1 Samuel 4-6

The Joy of Restoration

The people of Beth-shemesh were reaping their wheat harvest in the valley. And when they lifted up their eyes and saw the ark, they rejoiced to see it.

1 Samuel 6:13 esv

When the Philistines returned the ark of the covenant, there was rejoicing. The ark was where the powerful presence of God resided in those times, and it must have been both a relief and a powerful homecoming to have it back.

Restoration brings joy to waiting hearts. Thankfully, the powerful presence of God is not limited to a specific place. When Christ died, he removed what kept God separate from his people. There is no longer a need for God's presence to be protected. The Spirit of God resides in God's devoted followers. We have reason to rejoice in the restoration of our souls in God's presence!

Lord Jesus, thank you for tearing the veil in the temple and restoring right relationship with the Father through your sacrifice. I am yours, and I rejoice in knowing you!

Scripture Reading: 1 Samuel 7-9

Wholehearted Repentance

"If you are returning to the LORD with all your heart, get rid of the foreign gods and the Ashtoreths that are among you, set your hearts on the LORD, and worship only him. Then he will rescue you from the Philistines."

1 SAMUEL 7:3 CSB

Wholehearted repentance is not just saying "I'm sorry," and then going on our merry way. Repentance requires a turning: a return to the Lord. If we want to set ourselves up for success in following the Lord, we will not hold on any longer to the things that distract us from him. We lay aside all lesser loves, the things that keep us from living in the freedom of God's love.

When we set our hearts on the Lord and worship only him, our lives will show that. We don't claim to love him one moment and harbor hate against others the next. His ways become our ways, and we walk in the light of integrity.

Lord, I return to you today. You can have my whole heart. Show me the things that go against your kingdom ways, the things that detract from your love.

Scripture Reading: 1 Samuel 10-12

Called and Equipped

"Then the Spirit of the LORD will rush upon you, and you will prophesy with them and be changed into a different man."

1 SAMUEL 10:6 NASB

When God calls us, he also equips us. We don't have to know how we will do what he has called us to do; we surrender ourselves to his leadership and his grace empowers us in our weakness. We cannot control how the Lord will lead us or how he will move in our lives, but we can certainly surrender to his Spirit.

God's Word encourages us to trust in the Lord and follow him. He will do what we cannot! We have only to take each step he reveals, doing what is ours to do, and leave the rest to him. He not only moves on our behalf, but he transforms us in the power of his presence.

Spirit of the Lord, I trust you to do what I never could. I yield to your leadership in my life and trust you to bring me where you have called me.

Scripture Reading: 1 Samuel 13-15

Better than Sacrifice

"Has the LORD as great delight
in burnt offerings and sacrifices,
As in obeying the voice of the LORD?
Behold, to obey is better than sacrifice,
And to heed than the fat of rams."

1 SAMUEL 15:22 NKJV

God sees our hearts, and he recognizes our intentions. It is one thing to offer a sacrifice to appear holy. It is another thing to do what God asks us to do. God can't be fooled by outer expressions. He knows when we are resistant to his Word or trying to get out of following his ways.

Obedience is our greatest sacrifice, and it often costs us something. At the very least, it may cost us our pride. We cannot control or manipulate God with our sacrifice. He'd much rather have our obedience, and we'd be better off for it too.

Lord, I don't want to impress others with the sacrifices I make in your name. I want to know you, to follow you, and to choose the path of love at every turn.

Scripture Reading: 1 Samuel 16-18

The True You

"Don't look at how handsome Eliab is or how tall he is, because I have not chosen him. God does not see the same way people see. People look at the outside of a person, but the LORD looks at the heart."

1 SAMUEL 16:7 NCV

When Samuel went to the house of Jesse to find the next king of Israel, he found many strong and impressive men. But none of these were God's pick for king. His choice was a young shepherd who followed his ways and knew his heart. David was known as a man after God's own heart.

God isn't impressed by outer appearances. This is true of each of us. He sees our hearts. It doesn't matter how put-together we may seem, God is looking beyond our exterior. More than anything else, we can trust God with our hearts. He sees the tenderness and the strength, the vulnerability and the faith. Let's embrace who he says we are, and trust God's opinion is the greatest.

Lord, thank you for seeing the true me. I want to be more like you. Will you help me look past the outward appearance to see others from your perspective?

Scripture Reading: 1 Samuel 19-21

Friendship Matters

Jonathan said to David, "Go in peace, for we have sworn friendship with each other in the name of the LORD, saying, 'The LORD is witness between you and me, and between your descendants and my descendants forever.'"

1 SAMUEL 20:42 NIV

We don't need a lot of friends to feel seen, supported, and connected to others. David and Jonathan had a deep bond, and they agreed to have each other's backs. Considering who Jonathan's father was, that meant a lot.

A good friend is a relief and a strength in hard times. Proverbs 17:17 says, "A friend loves at all times." No friend is perfect, but they are willing to press through the hard times. We love each other by forgiving one another, giving grace, supporting each other in times of trouble, and by simply being there. Friendship is a gift from God!

Lord, thank you for friendship. I am grateful to not only have good friends in my life, but above all to have you as my closest and most faithful friend!

Scripture Reading: 1 Samuel 22-24

A Better Way

"May the LORD judge between us. Perhaps the LORD will punish you for what you are trying to do to me, but I will never harm you."

1 SAMUEL 24:12 NLT

The humble attitude of David in this passage is so much like Christ. Instead of demanding to be understood or taking vengeance into his own hands, he left the judgment up to God.

This is the way of God's kingdom. This is the path of love. May we choose the better way, just as David did. When faced with those who want to harm us, may we trust God to judge between us. He is our defender, he knows the truth, and he will bring it to light. Let's keep our hearts in God's love, and choose grace, standing firm in his powerful mercy.

Defender, thank you for this reminder today. You are the better way, and refusing to engage in harming others is the path of love. I trust you to do what you will.

Scripture Reading: 1 Samuel 25-27

Wise Counsel

David said to Abigail, "Blessed be the LORD, the God of Israel, who sent you this day to meet me! Blessed be your discretion, and blessed be you, who have kept me this day from bloodguilt and from working salvation with my own hand!"

1 SAMUEL 25:32-33 ESV

Abigail came to David as soon as she heard what her wicked husband had done. Meeting him before David could act on his own anger, she presented her case and prophesied God's faithfulness over him. It was a brave thing to do, and it was also what saved innocent men.

Wise counsel will protect you from acting in haste, and it will protect the innocent. May we offer wise counsel when it's in our ability to do so, and may we receive it when we need it.

Lord, your wisdom settles chaos and brings clarity to confusion. You are peace-giving, and you lead us into greater insight as we trust you.

Scripture Reading: 1 Samuel 28-31

Integrity Speaks

"As the Lord lives, you are an honorable man. I think it is good to have you fighting in this unit with me, because I have found no fault in you from the day you came to me until today."

1 Samuel 29:6 CSB

Achish was sure of David's character, even when the rulers over him didn't trust him. He had seen him in action, his character speaking louder than words. Just as David's integrity spoke to Achish, your character is what stands out to others.

Honorable characters always stand out. Many in this world would rather satisfy themselves than be known as reliable, loving, and true. Integrity means that our thoughts, words, and actions are genuine, sincere, and honest. They are aligned with God's Word and ways. Integrity always shines bright in a world filled with corruption.

Faithful One, I want my character to speak of your truth, love, and faithfulness. Thank you for transforming me as I follow your ways.

Scripture Reading: 2 Samuel 1-3

Honor and Grief

David took hold of his clothes and tore them, and so also did all the men who were with him. And they mourned and wept and fasted until evening for Saul and his son Jonathan.

2 SAMUEL 1:11-12 NASB

Personal victory can still leave room for honor and grief in another's loss. David mourned for the loss of his friend, but also for the loss of God's first anointed king over Israel. He didn't delight in the death of his enemy.

Love doesn't delight in destruction. While there may be relief and even joy at the prospect of peace, there is also a sense of grief over what was lost. True strength is in compassion. May we never be so blinded by our hurt that we can't see others for who they are. It is okay to fight for justice, to be grateful for it, and to also grieve what couldn't be or what wasn't.

Lord, may I take the time to honor and grieve what was lost, even as I enter into a new season of breakthrough.

Scripture Reading: 2 Samuel 4-6

Unabashed Praise

David danced before the Lord with all his might.
2 Samuel 6:14 NKJV

It was a day of rejoicing when the ark of the covenant was brought to Jerusalem. David didn't tone down his excitement by being solemn about it. He danced in the street with all his might! This wasn't in the privacy of his own home. He let his unabashed praise be seen by all.

In times of personal rejoicing, let's keep from toning it down. It is powerful to share our joy with others, and invite them into it. Some may choose to enter it with us, and others may remain on the outside of it, but what is worth celebrating is worth sharing! Let's let our praise, our wonder, and our gratitude be seen.

Lord, thank you for your faithfulness. I want to be as free as David was: to dance boldly and share the joy I have without toning it down when the occasion calls for it.

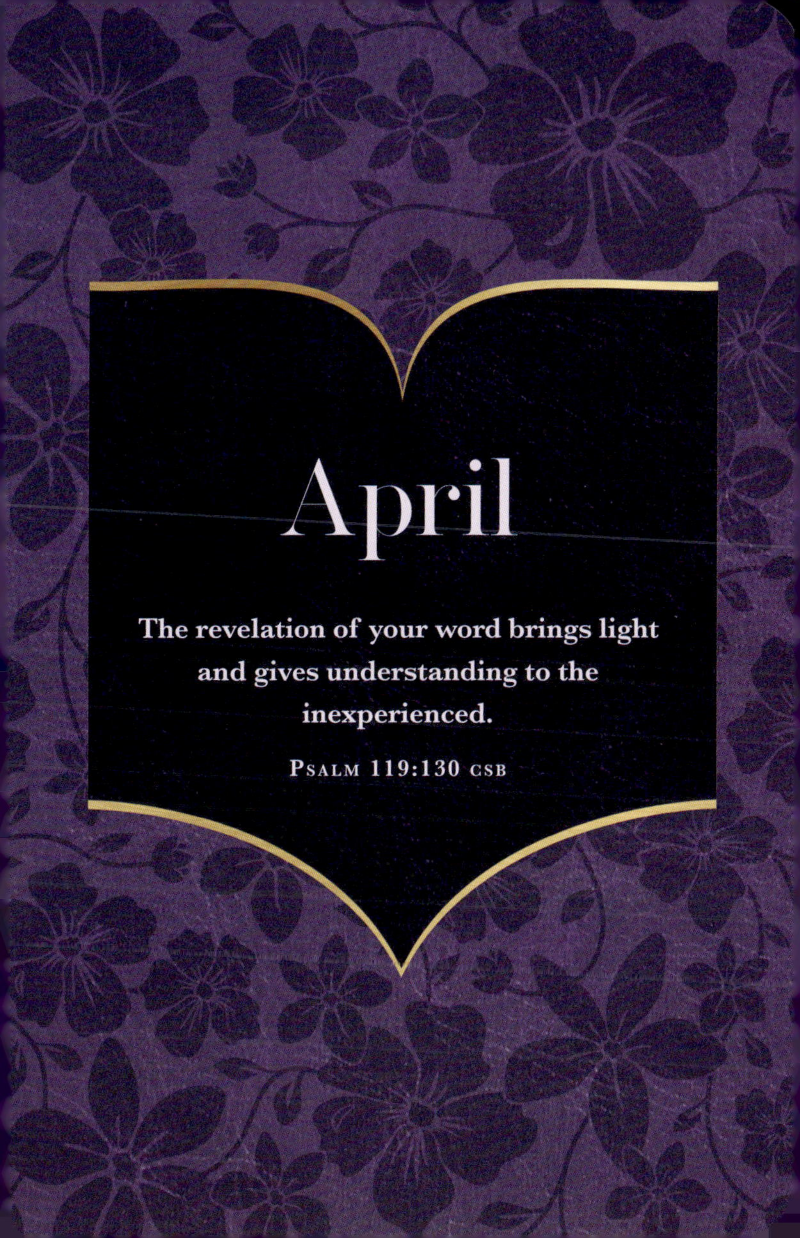
April
The revelation of your word brings light
and gives understanding to the
inexperienced.
Psalm 119:130 CSB

Scripture Reading: 2 Samuel 7-9

A Humble Heart

King David went in and sat in front of the LORD. David said, "LORD God, who am I? What is my family?"
2 SAMUEL 7:18 NCV

In response to Nathan's prophetic vision, David was overcome with gratitude. He didn't take for granted the favor of God over his life. He felt the wonder and awe of having been chosen by God and used to create a lineage of God's faithfulness.

As David sat before the Lord, his first words were, "Who am I? What is my family?" In his humble prayer, David recognized that there was nothing special about him that set him apart. But it was this humble heart that longed after God and followed through in bold faith that God desired. May we humble our hearts and remember that this is the place God is primarily after: our affection and devotion.

Lord, who am I that you would think of me? Who am I that you would choose me as your daughter? I'm so grateful to know you and be known by you.

Scripture Reading: 2 Samuel 10-12

What Is Good in His Sight

"Be strong, and let us fight bravely for our people and the cities of our God. The LORD will do what is good in his sight."

2 SAMUEL 10:12 NIV

Following the Lord isn't always easy. It's not all smooth paths and clear vision. Sometimes, the very thing required is what we struggle to embrace: courage and trust. There are no guaranteed outcomes in life, but we can trust God's promises. There isn't a need we have that he won't meet.

If you find yourself in a time where you're struggling with worry because you cannot control an outcome, this is your reminder that you're human, and that's part of the experience! Courage isn't needed when there's an absence of fear. Pray to the Lord, and then let your heart find rest in his faithfulness. You can trust him to do what is good in his sight.

Faithful One, meet me with your present peace and empower me in your gracious strength.

Scripture Reading: 2 Samuel 13-15

Let Yourself Feel

David walked up the road to the Mount of Olives, weeping as he went.

2 SAMUEL 15:30 NLT

David didn't try to hide his grief as he walked to the Mount of Olives. He openly wept, mourning with each step. We also don't need to hide our sorrow. God is close to the broken-hearted. He comforts all who mourn.

Somewhere along the line, taking time to grieve has been pushed out for the need to appear like we trust God. Beloved, we don't have to pretend with the Lord, and we shouldn't pretend with others either. Mourn with those who mourn. Sorrow is not a nuisance; it's a universal experience. Allowing ourselves to feel the sorrow that is present is as important as allowing others to freely express theirs. Let's let go of the lie that faith doesn't mourn. David wept. Jesus wept. Why shouldn't we?

Lord, thank you for the power of your presence in my sorrow. I don't want to dance around disappointment. I want you to meet me in it.

Scripture Reading: 2 Samuel 16-18

Standing Down

"It may be that the LORD will look on the wrong done to me, and that the LORD will repay me with good for his cursing today."

2 SAMUEL 16:12 ESV

We can't control what others think or say about us. We shouldn't try so hard to manage expectations that we lose sight of what truly matters. David's response to those cursing him wasn't to defend himself. It wasn't to show force in order to instill fear in those who opposed him. He left his defense to God, and we can do the same.

Let's not lose sleep over those who don't like us. Especially those who don't know us at all; it shouldn't matter what they think of us! This is easier said than done. Part of leaving it to God is letting go of the need to engage. Let's ask the Lord what he says of us, get reminders from those who know us well, and stand in the truth of that perspective.

Lord, help me to remember to keep the opinion of those who know me well above those who have loud opinions and little knowledge.

Scripture Reading: 2 Samuel 19-21

Mercy

"Should any man be killed in Israel today? Am I not aware that today I'm king over Israel?" So the king said to Shimei, "You will not die." Then the king gave him his oath.

2 SAMUEL 19:22-23 CSB

Mercy is a reflection of God's leadership. There is healing and restoration when powerful people extend the generosity of a second chance, no strings attached. While others might question our willingness to create a new start, when it is in our power to do so, let's choose the way of Christ.

Mercy is a powerful act that only the strong of faith can choose. It is much easier to choose self-righteousness. Still, God is our best example of mercy. He doesn't take delight in needless violence. He honors the humble, and he blesses those who walk in his ways.

Merciful One, your ways are not the ways of this world. May I walk in your ways and choose your love over my own self-righteousness.

Scripture Reading: 2 Samuel 22-24

Law of Love

David built there an altar to the LORD, and he offered burnt offerings and peace offerings. And the LORD responded to prayer for the land, and the plague was withdrawn from Israel.

2 SAMUEL 24:25 NASB

David was a man after God's own heart, but that doesn't mean he was perfect. He didn't choose God's ways every time. When he sinned, he didn't get away with it. The consequences of our actions are not God's judgment. They're an opportunity to turn in repentance and receive mercy.

God responds to the prayers of those who cry out to him in sincerity. We cannot expect to get it right every time. Instead of giving up, when we see the error of our ways and the effects it has on others, we have a choice to make. We can turn in humble repentance and be met with God's restorative mercy.

Lord, thank you for always keeping a path of restoration open in your merciful heart. I don't want to be so blinded by my own desires that I stop seeing what is right, good, merciful, and true.

Scripture Reading: 1 Kings 1-3

Seek Wisdom

"Therefore give to Your servant an understanding heart to judge Your people, that I may discern between good and evil. For who is able to judge this great people of Yours?"

1 KINGS 3:9 NKJV

Solomon did not take his ascent to leadership lightly. Rather than rule from a place of power and privilege, he humbled himself before the Lord, following in his father's footsteps. Solomon's prayer was not that he would have wealth or power, but wisdom.

Wisdom is a powerful treasure. It offers more than the influence of wealth. It produces more than the power of the world's governments. As Proverbs 8:11 says, "wisdom is better than rubies, and all the things one may desire cannot be compared with her." Wisdom's ways are worth pursuing, for it brings clarity, confidence, and a foundation of goodness to all who seek it.

Lord, Solomon saw the importance of seeking your wisdom, and so do I. Help me to walk in your ways and pursue your perspective.

Scripture Reading: 1 Kings 4-6

Sought and Answered

God gave Solomon great wisdom so he could understand many things… His wisdom was greater than any wisdom of the East, or any wisdom in Egypt.

1 Kings 4:29-30 NCV

God gave Solomon what he asked for, and even more, the whole nation was blessed for it. Wisdom was a pathway for honor, and the same is true for all who seek God's wisdom today. God's ways are uncomplicated. They are simple, but not always easy to choose.

The wisdom of God is exemplified in the life of Christ. 1 Corinthians 1:24 says, "Christ is the power of God and the wisdom of God." Wisdom becomes the foundation for a good life (though, that doesn't mean perfect). Let's seek first the kingdom of God and his righteousness, and remember that everything else will be added to that (Matthew 6:33).

Wise One, I choose to seek you first, and trust you for everything I can't account for. You are my provider, my wise counsel, my Savior, and my friend.

Scripture Reading: 1 Kings 7-9

Covenant Keeper

"LORD, the God of Israel, there is no God like you in heaven above or on earth below—you who keep your covenant of love with your servants who continue wholeheartedly in your way."

1 KINGS 8:23 NIV

God is faithful to his Word, and we can trust him to always do what he has promised. Our part? To trust him and wholeheartedly follow in his way. Again, the expectation of perfection isn't there. When we go off on our own way, he is ready to restore us when we return. Let's remember it's never too late to turn back to our faithful Father!

God is a covenant keeper. He is better than the best of men and women. Where we fail, he faithfully follows through. He is dependable and strong. He is powerful to save and to make a way where there is no way.

Faithful Father, thank you for the power of your love. You don't fail, and you never will. I will continue to turn to you.

Scripture Reading: 1 Kings 10-12

Empowered by Wisdom

"Praise the LORD your God, who delights in you and has placed you on the throne of Israel. Because of the LORD's eternal love for Israel, he has made you king so you can rule with justice and righteousness."

1 KINGS 10:9 NLT

Justice and righteousness are not born of power, they are born of wisdom. The wise person, as well as the wise leader, upholds righteousness and justice in their actions. Christ is our righteousness, holiness, and redemption. When we follow his ways, we uphold his wisdom in our lives.

Solomon's words in Proverbs 10 remind us that a life of godliness begins in the place of our hearts. "The words of the godly are a life-giving fountain; the words of the wicked conceal violent intentions" (verse eleven). Justice and righteousness reveal that wisdom is seated in our hearts. It is empowering to all who honor it with their actions.

Lord, you are the source of wisdom. You are just, righteous, and true. You don't compromise your love for power or self-satisfaction. You are beautiful in all your ways. May my life reflect the strength of your wisdom!

Scripture Reading: 1 Kings 13-15

In the Eyes of the Lord

Asa did what was right in the eyes of the LORD, as David his father had done.

1 KINGS 15:11 ESV

In the midst of rebellion, there were still people who followed the ways of the Lord. This is true today. Though wickedness is rampant, even in the Church, there is a remnant of people who follow wholeheartedly after the Lord.

Doing right in the eyes of the Lord will not always be the popular choice. It requires devotion, courage, and integrity. Thankfully, we have the grace of God to empower us in our weakness. As we rely on him, he moves through us. Willing hearts are better than empty shows of power. Let's make sure our hearts are right with the Lord, and keep our eyes on him every day.

Lord, I want to be one who does right in your sight, no matter what others think of me. There is so much noise distracting me from your love, but I choose you over and over again.

Scripture Reading: 1 Kings 16-18

Miraculous Provision

"The flour jar will not become empty and the oil jug will not run dry until the day the LORD sends rain on the surface of the land."

1 KINGS 17:14 CSB

The widow was willing to serve Elijah, even when she explained that she didn't have the means. Her willingness was met with miraculous provision. God took care of her by blessing what she had to never run out.

Do you trust that when you don't have means to help, God has the power to provide? Have you witnessed miracles of his goodness when you were at your end? In times of great need, we feel the desperation of it. This does not mean we've done anything wrong. God can meet us in our lack and provide creatively. He is able to do far more than we anticipate or imagine.

Miraculous One, I have questions, and I have needs. I ask you to meet me in them and to provide in ways I don't expect. Thank you.

Scripture Reading: 1 Kings 19-22

Rest and Receive

There was an angel touching him, and he said to him, "Arise, eat!" And he looked, and behold, there was at his head a round loaf of bread baked on hot coals, and a pitcher of water. So he ate and drank, and lay down again.

1 Kings 19:5-6 NASB

God takes care of our physical needs as well as our emotional and social needs. It is important that we not neglect what our bodies need, and sometimes that's just what Elijah needed: food, water, and rest!

If you find yourself exhausted, take your body's cues. Make time to rest and receive. Feed your body, water your soul, and sleep. We were created with limitations, and we can rest without shame for tending to those needs. God doesn't expect us to be superhuman! Receive what he offers today and rest in it.

Lord, help me to not neglect my physical needs. In a world that is endless with its demands, I choose to rest without guilt.

Scripture Reading: 2 Kings 1-3

God Is Present

Then he took the mantle of Elijah that had fallen from him, and struck the water, and said, "Where is the LORD God of Elijah?" And when he also had struck the water, it was divided this way and that; and Elisha crossed over.

2 KINGS 2:14 NKJV

As Elisha took the Elijah's mantle after it had fallen from him when he ascended into heaven on a chariot of fire, Elisha tested out the blessing he had asked for. He struck the water, asking "where is the Lord God of Elijah?" There was no audible response, but the answer was still clear: the water parted and he crossed over.

Having seen this, others noted that the spirit of Elijah rested on Elisha. He was already called and equipped. Now he just had to walk it out. When God calls us, he also equips us. He doesn't leave us when one of his beloved passes. He remains close. He remains faithful.

Lord, as you were with those who loved you, so you will be with me. Empower me with your Spirit, for I am surrendered to you.

Scripture Reading: 2 Kings 4-6

Faithful to Fill

When the jars were all full, she said to her son, "Bring me another jar." But he said, "There are no more jars." Then the oil stopped flowing.

2 Kings 4:6 NCV

God's power is generous. In miraculously filling multiple jars with oil until there was none left to fill, this widow was given a way to protect her sons and have a way to live. When we are in serious trouble, God is able to move on our behalf. It will not always mean sitting back and waiting. Sometimes, it will require us following a set of specific directions.

When we seek the Lord and an answer comes in an unexpected way, let's follow through in the way we're able. God will sometimes provide counsel through a wise friend. Other times, it may be an idea that hadn't occurred before. Let's be attentive, willing, and active in our pursuit of God's faithfulness.

Lord, give me wisdom and discernment when to wait on you and when to act on what I already know. I trust you to guide me and meet me with your goodness.

Scripture Reading: 2 Kings 7-9

Just You Wait

"Hear the word of the LORD. This is what the LORD says: About this time tomorrow, a seah of the finest flour will sell for a shekel and two seahs of barley for a shekel at the gate of Samaria."

2 KINGS 7:1 NIV

A day can change everything. Through Elisha, God revealed that the prices of food would go down significantly, meaning the siege would be lifted. God can cause things to shift quickly. If we find ourselves in a time of waiting, let's remember that God's timing is perfect. He doesn't ignore the cries of his people.

Circumstances can shift overnight. Let's trust God to move and lead us in those times. While we wait, we can trust him to protect and provide. God is present in stillness and in movement. There isn't a moment when we are without him!

Faithful God, I trust you in the waiting, and I trust you in swift changes. Be near, and keep me close to your heart through it all.

Scripture Reading: 2 Kings 10-12

Honest and Trustworthy

No accounting of this money was required from the construction supervisors, because they were honest and trustworthy men.

2 Kings 12:15 NLT

A trustworthy person is worth their weight in gold! While some look for ways to cut corners and increase their bottom line, an honest and trustworthy person does what they say they will in the way they promise to do it.

It is good to be known as honest and reliable. These are powerful character traits that enhance a reputation. It is much better to be known in this way than to have lots of wealth and influence with little respect. When we walk in integrity, there's no need to keep things hidden.

Lord, as you are honest and trustworthy, I hope to be too. May I be a woman of my word instead of trying to please others.

Scripture Reading: 2 Kings 13-15

Covenant of Compassion

The LORD was gracious to them and had compassion on them, and he turned toward them, because of his covenant with Abraham, Isaac, and Jacob.

2 KINGS 13:23 ESV

God is faithful even when we're not. His covenant is stronger than our failures. Some kings of Israel chose to serve him and some did not. His faithfulness remained intact. We can trust God to do what he has promised. He will never go back on his covenant of compassion or turn from the power of his mercy.

God is the same yesterday, today, and forever. He continues to move in our generation, and we can trust his love to deliver us from our fears as we put our hope in him. It doesn't matter how often we fail or forget. God is ready to receive and restore us.

Lord, I don't want to take your faithful love for granted. Remind me when I stray that you are ready to receive me as I am.

Scripture Reading: 2 Kings 16-18

Unparalleled Trust

Hezekiah relied on the LORD God of Israel; not one of the kings of Judah was like him, either before him or after him. He remained faithful to the LORD and did not turn from following him but kept the commands the LORD had commanded Moses.

2 KINGS 18:5-6 CSB

King Hezekiah wasn't only godly. He remained faithful to the Lord in his entire reign. This could not be said of any king that came before or after. Still imperfect, he nevertheless was devoted to following the law of the Lord and upholding it in the kingdom.

When we come to the end of our lives, what will matter most is how we lived: how we spent our time and what we gave our attention to. We don't have to wait until the end to wonder who we could have been. Let's be faithful in our own lives, no matter how little they seem to us. Our character can have a lasting impact.

Lord, I trust you, and I want my life to reflect it. Be honored in my heart, work, and relationships.

Scripture Reading: 2 Kings 19-20

Bring Your Burdens

Hezekiah… went up to the house of the LORD and spread it out before the LORD. Hezekiah prayed before the LORD.

2 KINGS 19:14-15 NASB

Hezekiah took his fears and laid them before the altar of God. He prayed for his mercy and intervention. When we have heavy burdens, we can also bring them before the Lord and lay them at his throne.

It does us no good to sit in our fear. Why would we stay in that place when we have access to the King of Kings and Lord of Lords? He is the one who can move in miraculous power and shift things we don't even see. We don't have to know how God will help us in order to ask him to do just that.

God my help, you are the one who settles my soul in the peace of your presence and sets the record straight on my account. There are many reasons to fear in this day and age, but I bring them all to you.

Scripture Reading: 2 Kings 21-23

Faith-filled Action

The king commanded Hilkiah the high priest, the priests of the second order, and the doorkeepers, to bring out of the temple of the LORD all the articles that were made for Baal.

2 KINGS 23:4 NKJV

Josiah didn't just pledge his devotion to the Lord, he followed through with faith-filled action. He removed the idols, took down the high places erected to other gods, and cleaned out the temple by removing those who didn't honor the one true God.

It is one thing to say we love and follow God. It is another thing to put that into obvious action. Our choices reflect what we believe, whether we put intention behind them or not. Faith without action is empty, but the fruit of God's Spirit is evident in the lives of those who truly follow his path.

Lord, I don't want your love to be a question in my life. I choose to follow you, and to put your ways above my own.

Scripture Reading: 2 Kings 24-25

Spark of Hope

Evil-Merodach spoke kindly to Jehoiachin and gave him a seat of honor above the seats of the other kings who were with him in Babylon. So Jehoiachin put away his prison clothes.

2 Kings 25:28-29 NCV

Even in incredibly hard times, God offers a spark of hope. Jehoiachin was freed from his prison sentence in Babylon and given a place of honor at the table of the evil king. Even though he had suffered for thirty-seven years in prison, at the end of his life, he was honored.

Suffering does not last forever. Even a spark of hope can remind us of the goodness of God. Let's look to him, no matter how hard things get. He is faithful to be with us and to restore us as we turn to him.

Lord, I ask for a spark of hope today to see where you are in my world. I know that your faithful mercy is always at work in the details. Give me eyes to see a glimpse of your kindness today.

Scripture Reading: 1 Chronicles 1-3

Women Honored

Shammua, Shobab, Nathan and Solomon. These four were by Bathsheba daughter of Ammiel.

1 CHRONICLES 3:5 NIV

Though much of the lineage listed in Chronicles is focused on men, there are over fifty women listed as well. God does not overlook women or their role in his kingdom. Bathsheba didn't have much of a choice in her relationship with King David, but she was honored as a mother to four sons, including King Solomon.

We can't always control the situations we end up in, but we can choose to make the best with what we've got. Let's not give into the lie that our lives are lesser than any other. As we choose to live with love, integrity, and grace, we can walk in the confidence of our identity in Christ. He always honors our hearts, even when others overlook them.

Lord, thank you for your kindness. Empower me to love well. You see and honor what others miss. Thank you.

Scripture Reading: 1 Chronicles 4-6

Cry for Expansion

Jabez cried out to the God of Israel, "Oh, that you would bless me and enlarge my territory! Let your hand be with me, and keep me from harm so that I will be free from pain." And God granted his request.

1 Chronicles 4:10 NLT

Jabez was known as an honorable man (or at the very least more honorable than his brothers). When he cried to the Lord for expansion and his hand of blessing, God answered. What a bold thing to pray!

When we humble our hearts before God, we don't have to keep ourselves from asking for God's favor. He knows us already and delights in giving good gifts to his children. Let's not withhold our earnest prayers from the one who loves to meet us. Go ahead, pray for the greater things today, and trust God with the answer.

God, that you would bless me and expand my territory. With your hand as my guide, keep me close and in your love. Be glorified in my life.

Scripture Reading: 1 Chronicles 7-9

City Builder

His daughter was Sheerah, who built both Lower and Upper Beth-horon, and Uzzen-sheerah.

1 Chronicles 7:24 ESV

In a sea of men and their accomplishments, Sheerah stands out as a notable exception. She wasn't referred to as a mother, but as a city builder. It is not only men that build communities; women are just as active in this pursuit, though few get recognition.

As women, our identities are not only in our relationships as daughters, sisters, mothers, or friends. We have more to offer this world than our wombs. We can lead as Deborah did, fight as Jael did, build cities as Sheerah did, and leave a lasting legacy. Our gifts need not go unused in Christ's kingdom. He welcomed women as well as men to follow him, and he welcomes you today.

Lord, thank you for the reminder that my place in your kingdom is not as a second-class citizen. I am a daughter, and I get to partner with your kingdom and build in your name.

Scripture Reading: 1 Chronicles 10-12

Strength of Strategy

From the Issacharites, who understood the times and knew what Israel should do: 200 chiefs with all their relatives under their command.

1 CHRONICLES 12:32 CSB

David had support from many soldiers and powerful people for his leadership over Israel. Not only that, but he also had wise strategists who understood God's timing and had practical insights for what needed to be done. How invaluable that was to David, and how important it is that we also have access to wise and discerning people.

God gives wisdom to those who seek it. If we want to understand his timing, and we ask for his wisdom to do just that, he will offer it. Let's be sure to seek God for his wisdom and listen to the grounded strategy of discerning people who display the character of wisdom in their own lives.

Wise God, wisdom is like a treasure, and I want to find it. There is so much power in perspective, and I'd rather see from yours than my limited view.

Scripture Reading: 1 Chronicles 13-15

Prioritize Presence

"Let us bring back the ark of our God to us, since we did not seek it in the days of Saul."

1 CHRONICLES 13:3 NASB

God's guidance had been a missing factor in Israel's leadership during the last part of Saul's reign. David recognized that it was important to bring the ark of God's presence back. It was no small thing to do, but it was vital to the kingdom.

We don't have to do a pilgrimage to return to the presence of God. He is already near and ready to receive us as we return to him. The Holy Spirit is not bound to a physical space. God's Spirit is able to move freely in and through us, and as we turn our hearts toward the Lord and prioritize his presence once more, we are flooded with his peace and overwhelming love.

Lord, before I do anything else today, I prioritize your presence. Meet me in this place.

Scripture Reading: 1 Chronicles 16-18

God Flips the Script

"Go and tell My servant David, 'Thus says the LORD: "You shall not build Me a house to dwell in"… Furthermore I tell you that the LORD will build you a house.'"

1 CHRONICLES 17:4,10 NKJV

God's presence had been moving from tent to tent with the people as they moved. But there would come a time when God would settle his people. David wanted to build God a house, a permanent dwelling place, but God said that it was not his job, though it would be a part of his legacy.

What's remarkable, beautiful, and so like God is that he took what David proposed and promised to do the same for him. He would build David a house! How often do we say to the Lord, I'm going to do this for you, and then he flips the script and does it for us? It is his way to bless us in ways that we don't anticipate and yet astound us.

Lord, even when I am not able to do what I want for you, you overwhelm me with your gifts of goodness. You are so good to me.

Scripture Reading: 1 Chronicles 19-21

Costly Offering

King David answered Araunah, "No, I will pay the full price for the land. I won't take anything that is yours and give it to the LORD. I won't offer a burnt offering that costs me nothing."

1 CHRONICLES 21:24 NCV

David was desperate for God's mercy, knowing he had done wrong in the sight of God. Watching others pay the price for his sin didn't harden him; it moved him in desperation to seek God's mercy. When Araunah offered his threshing floor to the king for free, David refused. He wouldn't offer God something that cost him nothing.

When we take personal responsibility for our actions, it's important that in the restoration, we also use that accountability: that it cost us something. It's not easy to admit when we're wrong and then do the work to seek restoration. It will cost us, but the return will be worth it, and our character will be strengthened in the process.

Lord, I know I'm not helpless in my own life, and I'm not a victim to my circumstances. I take responsibility for what is mine, and I trust you with the rest.

Scripture Reading: 1 Chronicles 22-24

Devotion Leads to Direction

"Devote your heart and soul to seeking the LORD your God. Begin to build the sanctuary of the LORD God, so that you may bring the ark of the covenant of the LORD and the sacred articles belonging to God into the temple that will be built for the Name of the LORD."

1 CHRONICLES 22:19 NIV

David's encouragement to his son, Solomon, was that he devote his heart and soul to seeking the Lord. This was the primary goal. Then he would begin to build the sanctuary of the temple for the Lord's presence. Devotion to the Lord leads to direction as we build.

Today's verse echoes Jesus' statement in Matthew 6:33, "Seek first his kingdom and righteousness, and all these things will be given to you as well." Not only will you have what you need when you devote your life to the Lord, but you will also have wisdom to guide you.

Lord, my greatest aim is to be devoted to you with my whole heart. I seek you first.

May

Let the word of Christ dwell richly among you, in all wisdom teaching and admonishing one another through psalms, hymns, and spiritual songs, singing to God with gratitude in your hearts.

Colossians 3:16 csb

Scripture Reading: 1 Chronicles 25-27

Prophetic Worship

David and the army commanders then appointed men from the families of Asaph, Heman, and Jeduthun to proclaim God's messages to the accompaniment of lyres, harps, and cymbals.

1 Chronicles 25:1 NLT

Music is a powerful way to engage with the message of the Lord. The messages of God's nature, his ways, and his faithfulness sink deep with skilled hands and voices, beautiful melodies, and powerful rhythms.

When we proclaim God's messages, we are prophetic voices. When we receive them, we are opening our hearts to God's powerful Word. God loves to move through the creative gifts of his people. Let's not ignore how powerful the arts are to our walk with God. Put on some music or make some to praise the Lord today!

Lord, you are worthy of worship, and music is a wonderful way to offer you my attention. As I praise you today, meet me with the power of your presence.

Scripture Reading: 1 Chronicles 28-29

Searcher of Hearts

"You, Solomon my son, know the God of your father and serve him with a whole heart and with a willing mind, for the LORD searches all hearts and understands every plan and thought."

1 CHRONICLES 28:9 ESV

God is the searcher of all hearts. He understands our intentions better than we do. He sees what's behind every plan and thought. This might be a fearful thought to those who only want to please themselves and bring harm to others, but it is freedom to those who humble themselves before him. He knows where we come from, and he knows where we are going. When we devote ourselves to loving and following the Lord, we have nothing to fear.

God can change our hearts. He removes the hardness and softens us in the power of his love. We can trust him to do this work as we devote our hearts and minds to him!

Lord, search my heart and know me. Transform me from the inside out.

Scripture Reading: 2 Chronicles 1-3

Above and Beyond

"Wisdom and knowledge are given to you. I will also give you riches, wealth, and glory, unlike what was given to the kings who were before you, or will be given to those after you."

2 Chronicles 1:12 csb

All Solomon asked the Lord for was wisdom, but God promised him that and so much more. God goes above and beyond what we ask him to do when we seek him wholeheartedly. He is inherently generous.

Asking God for wisdom leads to a full life. Wisdom isn't just a theory, it is endlessly practical. When Solomon asked God for wisdom, he was asking to know how the Lord would lead his people. When we ask God for wisdom, it's not only to succeed in what we do, but to do it exceedingly well.

Wise God, you are so generous! The more I know you the more I love you, the more I trust you, and the more I want to serve you.

Scripture Reading: 2 Chronicles 4-6

God's Greatness

"Will God really dwell with mankind on the earth? Behold, heaven and the highest heaven cannot contain You; how much less this house which I have built!"

2 Chronicles 6:18 NASB

God cannot be contained, and Solomon knew this even as he built a sanctuary to welcome his presence. We might feel the same way as God's living temples (2 Corinthians 6:16). God is everywhere, and yet he chooses to also dwell in his people. We cannot escape his presence, no matter where on the earth we roam, for he is with us.

God's greatness is beyond our comprehension, and yet he gives us glorious glimpses through the revelation of his Word. What a wonderful mystery it is to know God is greater than everything in this world, and yet he chooses to dwell in us.

Lord, expand my understanding of your glory and greatness today.

Scripture Reading: 2 Chronicles 7-9

Humble Hearts

"If My people who are called by My name will humble themselves, and pray and seek My face, and turn from their wicked ways, then I will hear from heaven, and will forgive their sin and heal their land."

2 CHRONICLES 7:14 NKJV

It takes humility to admit when we're wrong. Pride is not strength; it's weakness. A humble heart is a teachable heart, and that matters more than proving ourselves. God invites us to turn to him with humility and seek his ways when we find ourselves in messes of our own making. It is better to readily humble ourselves and turn to him than prolong our suffering with obstinate pride.

God is ready to forgive, heal, and restore the repentant heart. He will set right what we mishandle ourselves, and will teach us a better way. If we long for healing, let's turn to the Lord. If we long for peace, he's the one to go to. If we long for a better way, he is the way, the truth, and the life.

Lord, I humble my heart before you. Do what only you can do.

Scripture Reading: 2 Chronicles 10-12

Kindness Matters

"Be kind to these people. If you please them and give them a kind answer, they will serve you always."

2 Chronicles 10:7

Godly leadership is rooted in kindness and humility, not in threats or coercion. King Rehoboam rejected the wise advice and instead chose to follow in his father's footsteps by being needlessly harsh. He drove many in Israel away.

Kindness goes a long way in earning trust. It shows respect of fellow humanity and leaves room for partnership. Power-hungry people often reject this way of leadership, for their concern is in getting their own way. May we be people who choose kindness and humility in our interactions. It is always the better path, and it really is the only wise choice if we want to work well with others.

Lord, you are kind. No matter what kind of people are in power, you are better, truer, and your ways are worth following.

Scripture Reading: 2 Chronicles 13-15

Powerful Help

Asa called to the LORD his God and said, "LORD, there is no one like you to help the powerless against the mighty. Help us, LORD our God, for we rely on you."
2 CHRONICLES 14:11 NIV

Have you ever felt like your back was up against the wall and you couldn't find a way out? This is what Asa and Judah were facing. The odds were stacked against them, and their only hope was the Lord.

When we find ourselves in desperate circumstances, let's turn to the Lord who readily helps those who rely on him. Asa was a good and godly king. He took down idols and encouraged his people to seek the Lord. When he cried out for the Lord's help, it was built upon a history of faithfulness. Let's build our own lives of devotion to the Lord and reach out in our need. He is faithful to answer.

Lord, you are a powerful help to all who cry to you. I want to know you, to love you, and to follow you through easy times as well as the hard.

Scripture Reading: 2 Chronicles 16-18

Gracious Strength

"The eyes of the LORD search the whole earth in order to strengthen those whose hearts are fully committed to him."

2 CHRONICLES 16:9 NLT

God faithfully strengthens those who set their hearts on him. When we are devoted to the Lord and committed to walking in his ways, his grace is present even before we know to ask for help. God is our strength, so let's not get distracted by the empty promises of others. Let's always pursue his counsel!

More than anything, if we set our hearts on loving the Lord and following his ways, we will always have his strength. There won't be a moment where we are without it. Let's devote our strength to the Lord and trust him to strengthen us where we are weak.

Lord, I need you more than I rely on my own strength. You are my God, and I want to honor you with every part of my life.

Scripture Reading: 2 Chronicles 19-21

Eyes on God

"We do not know what to do, but our eyes are on you."
2 CHRONICLES 20:12 ESV

As all of Judah stood before the Lord, the Spirit of the Lord moved and spoke. "Listen, all Judah and inhabitants of Jerusalem… 'Do not be afraid and do not be dismayed at this great horde, for the battle is not yours but God's.'" When the people turned to God for help, he assured them that he would move on their behalf.

When we don't know what to do, let's not wallow in fear. It's the perfect opportunity to take our fears and turn our attention to the Lord, bringing them before him. God does not ridicule us when we don't know what to do! He offers to fight for us. There is no greater assurance than God's powerful help.

Lord, I don't want to wait even a moment before I bring my uncertainty and confusion to you. You always have a plan. My eyes are on you in expectant hope.

Scripture Reading: 2 Chronicles 22-24

Quiet Courage

Jehoshabeath, the king's daughter, rescued Joash son of Ahaziah… Since she was Ahaziah's sister, she hid Joash from Athaliah so that she did not kill him.

2 Chronicles 22:11 csb

The king's daughter was quietly courageous. Not all courage needs to be seen by others. Much of it happens behind closed doors for no one (or few) to witness. Courageous character doesn't need an audience. It does what is right and does what it can.

Take heart in knowing God sees and honors your acts of quiet courage. When no one else recognizes what you are doing, it doesn't make it any less notable. God honors sacrifices of courage done in secret, and he brings blessing. Remember his audience is the only one that matters.

Lord, thank you for the reminder that every act of courage, integrity, and mercy matters. I choose to live my life for you.

Scripture Reading: 2 Chronicles 25-27

Direct Your Ways

Jotham became powerful because he directed his ways before the LORD his God.

2 CHRONICLES 27:6 NASB

We are not victims to our circumstances or the way we have done things up until this point. We can change our minds and change our course. If we have it in our hearts to do things differently, we will take steps to choose a new way.

When we follow God, he directs us. He leads us in faithful love and grows us in his truth, mercy, and wisdom. The more we get to know God, the more we see how wonderful he is. His nature is more beautiful than we can imagine, and his power is awe-inducing. Let's direct our hearts, minds, and lives before the Lord, and he will transform us in his living love.

Lord, I don't want to stay stuck in cycles of fear, shame, or sin. Lead me into your love as I direct my heart, mind, and actions in your ways.

Scripture Reading: 2 Chronicles 28-30

Readied by God

Hezekiah and all the people rejoiced that God had prepared the people, since the events took place so suddenly.

2 Chronicles 29:36 NKJV

God prepares us for transitions, and we can trust that his guidance has purpose. What we've been waiting for can quickly happen when the time is right. We don't know exactly when God will move, but as he leads, we can trust we'll be ready.

God is purposeful in his preparation. When we can't see the full picture, let's trust the one who puts it all together. There isn't a detail he misses. His faithful mercy weaves everything together in a grand tapestry of his goodness.

Lord, thank you for the power of your thoughtfulness and mercy that prepare me for what's to come. I trust you to equip me and ready my life for what you are doing.

Scripture Reading: 2 Chronicles 31-33

The Power of Generosity

"Since the people began to bring their offerings to the Temple of the LORD, we have had plenty to eat and plenty left over, because the LORD has blessed his people. So we have all this left over."

2 CHRONICLES 31:10 NCV

Generosity leads to abundance. When God's people bring heartfelt offerings to the Lord, it blesses the community. Generosity is a sign of God's love alive and well, pouring out of his people.

Gratitude leads us in generosity. When we understand who God is, and the power of his generosity toward us, what response is there but to offer back to him a portion of what he has so freely given us? The Lord is limitless in love, and his grace is available in every moment. We have more than enough, so we don't have to hoard what we have. As we share from a place of receptivity and reciprocity, no one is left without.

Lord, I want to be generous as you are generous . There is so much power when your people freely offer their gifts and resources to you and others.

Scripture Reading: 2 Chronicles 34-36

True Conviction

When the king heard the words of the Law, he tore his robes. "Because your heart was responsive and you humbled yourself before God… I have heard you," declares the LORD.

2 CHRONICLES 34:19,27 NIV

Conviction—or the realization of the wrong we've done—is a powerful agent for change. When our hearts are pierced with the truth, it is an opportunity to humble ourselves and turn to the Lord in repentance. We don't have to continue just because that's what we've been doing.

God's kindness leads us to repentance. His truth does not crush us, though it does pierce us from time to time. The pain of that drives us to the Lord to be set right, reconciled, and forgiven. He pays attention to those who call on his name. Let's not stay away for fear of how we'll be received. He forgives us as many times as we come to him with a humble heart and willingness to change.

Lord, I don't want to ignore the pangs of your truth when they knock on the door of my heart. Set my mind and heart right in the truth of who you are.

Scripture Reading: Ezra 1-3

Stirred by God

God stirred the hearts of the priests and Levites and the leaders of the tribes of Judah and Benjamin to go to Jerusalem to rebuild the Temple of the LORD.

EZRA 1:5 NLT

God moves in the hearts of people to do his work. If you've ever felt stirred to do something for the Lord, you don't have to question it. Sure, not every idea is one that you act on, but the ones you can't shake off are worth noting.

Is there a stirring that God has put in you? Is it for creative work, an interesting hobby, or a people group? God uses all sorts of things to bring honor to his kingdom. Those little movements toward curiosity, care, and creativity are worth exploring.

Creator, you made me in your image, and that makes me a creative person. As I explore what you have already been stirring, be honored as I follow you in it.

Scripture Reading: Ezra 4-6

Favorable Change

They kept the Feast of Unleavened Bread seven days with joy, for the LORD had made them joyful and had turned the heart of the king of Assyria to them, so that he aided them in the work of the house of God, the God of Israel.

EZRA 6:22 ESV

God is able to change hearts. His people rejoiced and feasted in celebration, for he had given them favor under the king of Assyria. Not only had God turned his heart, but he helped them in the work of the house of God. A reason to rejoice!

When people are opposed to us, it can feel discouraging. Let's not give up hope. As we keep doing what we know to do and trusting the Lord to open doors, he will do what only he can do. Whether that's a changed heart or a creative alternative, he always makes a way for his people!

Lord, you are faithful, powerful, and always there when I need you. I rejoice in your love that never leaves or forsakes me!

Scripture Reading: Ezra 7-10

Glimmer of Hope

"We have been unfaithful to our God... but there is still hope for Israel in spite of this."

EZRA 10:2 CSB

In God, no matter how much we've failed or gone our own way, there is always hope. Jesus Christ is our living hope, our redemption, and our way forward. He restores what was broken and makes us whole in him.

If we will humble ourselves before the Lord and turn to him, he will forgive us our debts, and release us from the weight of shame, sin, and fear. He is better than the judges of this earth, and his justice remains unwavering. In Christ, we are healed, delivered, and liberated. We become new in his mercy, and he never holds our past against us. This is more than a glimmer of hope we have today. It is a bright, shining beacon!

Jesus Christ, you are my living hope. Thank you for the promise of redemption, restoration, and release in your merciful forgiveness.

Scripture Reading: Nehemiah 1-3

A Bold Ask

The king granted them to me because the good hand of my God was on me.

NEHEMIAH 2:8 NASB

When the king asked Nehemiah why he was sad, he replied honestly. The king in turn asked what he could do. Nehemiah took a moment to pray and then made a bold ask: permission to return to his land to rebuild what had been destroyed.

When others see our need, we don't have to hide it. Let's have the courage to speak the truth, and when they ask how they can help, prayerfully consider it. Even if what we need feels like a stretch, we can boldly ask for what God has placed on our hearts.

Lord, thank you for seeing me and putting me in places of connection where there are people to rely on. As far as I can, may I support those who need it.

Scripture Reading: Nehemiah 4-6

Singular Focus

"I am doing a great work, so that I cannot come down."
NEHEMIAH 6:3 NKJV

Nehemiah's focus protected him against those who wanted to do him harm. He knew the work he had to do, and he focused on doing it with all his strength. God honors devotion, and he protects us in it.

Though the people trying to coax him used fear to intimidate, God strengthened his hands to finish the work he set out to do. This was an ambitious work, for the wall was finished in only fifty-two days. This was so impressive it was seen as an act of God! When we partner with God's work, he increases our efforts and reveals his glory. Let's stay focused on what we have to do, and not be distracted by the efforts of others to pull us away from it.

Lord, I don't need to be concerned with what others are doing or want me to do; I know what you have put before me. Be in it with me and bless it.

Scripture Reading: Nehemiah 7-9

Joyful Strength

"Go and enjoy good food and sweet drinks. Send some to people who have none, because today is a holy day to the Lord. Don't be sad, because the joy of the Lord will make you strong."

Nehemiah 8:10 NCV

The joy of the Lord makes us strong. Ah, what a familiar refrain! In song form, short meditation, or timely reminder, the strength of joy is a powerful medicine. We don't have to be serious all the time, or deprive ourselves of good fellowship or celebratory foods. Let's embrace times of joy and know that we are stronger for it!

Wherever you find yourself today, may you be filled with the joy of the Lord. His presence is close, and the fruit of his Spirit is not only patience and self-control. It is also joy! Rejoice in the Lord, for he has given this day to you with all its gifts.

Father, I rejoice in your love. Fill me to overflowing with your joy!

Scripture Reading: Nehemiah 10-11

Willingness to Serve

The people commended all who volunteered to live in Jerusalem.

NEHEMIAH 11:2 NIV

It is a big deal to be willing to leave comfort to serve the Lord. Obedience is powerful, but willing surrender is a testimony of wholehearted devotion. God blesses the choices we make to honor him.

Volunteering is a beautiful way to exemplify servanthood. It cannot be coerced. It is something that we willingly do for the betterment of our communities. Is there something you feel led to volunteer to do to further God's kingdom? Don't hesitate. It's an honor and a powerful testimony of God's goodness.

Lord, thank you for the reminder that getting out of my comfort zone is a good thing. Open my eyes to ways I can serve you and support those who are already doing your work.

Scripture Reading: Nehemiah 12-13

Sing for Joy

Many sacrifices were offered on that joyous day, for God had given the people cause for great joy. The women and children also participated in the celebration, and the joy of the people of Jerusalem could be heard far away.

NEHEMIAH 12:43 NLT

When we have reason to celebrate, let's not hold back! It is right that we sing for joy, make a feast of it, and share it with others. The joy of God's people could be heard for miles. Can you imagine what a loud party that must have been?

We are not meant to live so seriously that we forget to take advantage of joy when it presents itself. Let's not neglect gathering together to celebrate one another, and to celebrate what God has done. It is right, good, and powerful to let our joy be seen.

Lord, you are the joy-giver. I don't want to hold back my songs of praise for what you have done. I celebrate your presence with me, and your powerful hand of mercy over my life.

Scripture Reading: Esther 1-3

Open Doors

Esther was winning favor in the eyes of all who saw her.
ESTHER 2:15 ESV

The Lord opens doors that no one else can. When he puts his hand of favor on you, you will find yourself in places you could not have entered on your own. He is wise, and he knows what he is doing. You can trust him to open the right doors at the right time.

What is your responsibility in this? Trust the Lord and follow his ways. He will shine through you as you dedicate your heart to his nature. The fruit of the Spirit will be evident in your life as you develop your character. It wasn't just Esther's beauty that gave her favor with the king and his court; it was the strength and beauty of her character.

Lord, I want my character to look like yours. You are my leader, and I trust you to open doors at the right time in a way that only you can.

Scripture Reading: Esther 4-6

This Present Moment

"Perhaps you have come to your royal position for such a time as this."

Esther 4:14 CSB

There is power in the place you are in right now. You can't go back to fix the past or jump ahead to what's to come. The present is all you have, and it is enough! It is enough to know the power of God in your life. He is palpable in the mundane as you turn your attention to him. He is actively weaving mercy into the details of your life.

Here in this place there is opportunity for you to serve the Lord. He has given you a voice and a perspective. Will you yield your heart to him and follow his lead?

Faithful One, even when things feel hard, I know that you are with me. Show me the power of your presence here in this place.

Scripture Reading: Esther 7-8

The Power of Influence

"If I have found favor in your sight, O king, and if it pleases the king, let my life be given me as my request, and my people as my wish."

ESTHER 7:3 NASB

Esther had the ear of the king, but that didn't mean she knew what his response would be. She very literally took her life into her hands by speaking up in this way. Still, she counted the cost and found that it was worth it.

When we are in places of influence, may we refrain from protecting ourselves at the stake of harming others. It's a tempting place to be: to remain in the comfort of our own favor. But it's much more important that we stand for the vulnerable and speak up for those who don't have a voice in the spaces we inhabit.

Lord, I don't want to keep from speaking up for what is right to protect my own comfort. Help me to be bold and strong, standing on truth.

Scripture Reading: Esther 9-10

From Sorrow to Joy

The month which was turned from sorrow to joy for them, and from mourning to a holiday; that they should make them days of feasting and joy.

ESTHER 9:22 NKJV

What was meant to harm God's people was turned around. God turned their sorrow to overwhelming joy as the tables were turned. When we can see no way out of our situation, it doesn't mean that we're doomed.

Let's trust God to turn sorrow into joy. Psalm 30:11 is a powerful praise when he does! "You have turned my mourning into dancing; you have put off my sackcloth and clothed me with gladness."

Lord, you make a way where no one else can. You turn cause for sorrow into celebration, and you give the garment of praise in place of heaviness.

Scripture Reading: Job 1-4

Praise Regardless

"The LORD gave these things to me,
and he has taken them away.
Praise the name of the LORD."
JOB 1:21 NCV

No matter the situation we are facing, we can choose to praise the Lord. When he gives, we praise him. When he takes away, we praise him still. There isn't a moment we're without his presence, and it is his grace that strengthens us in weakness.

It is easy to praise the Lord when all is going well. It is much more difficult when everything falls apart. Different circumstances, same God. He hasn't changed. He is still faithful, just, and true. When our faith is tested, God remains faithful! Praise God even when it's hard, when you don't understand, and when you're in the midst of the battle.

Lord, I offer you my sacrifice of praise when things are hard. Be near in it all.

Scripture Reading: Job 5-8

Lifted Up

The lowly he sets on high,
and those who mourn are lifted to safety.
JOB 5:11 NIV

God meets us in our pain. He doesn't leave us brokenhearted. He comes close in comfort, lifts us up, and brings us into the safety of his presence. He doesn't abandon the weak.

When we are feeling low, Jesus is our hope. He is our comfort and peace. There is no pain so great he can't get close to us and heal us. Sorrow is not a sin. Neither is suffering. Jesus experienced both. Instead of trying to escape our sadness, why don't we invite him into it? It's the very place he wants to minister to and heal as he wraps us in his loving arms.

Comforter, when I can't see for the sadness, press in close in the power of your presence. In times of peace, may I be a comfort to others as you have been to me.

Scripture Reading: Job 9-12

Unable to See

He does great things too marvelous to understand.
He performs countless miracles.
Yet when he comes near, I cannot see him.
When he moves by, I do not see him go.
Job 9:10-11 NLT

Job knew God well. He had followed him devotedly, and he knew his nature. Even in the midst of his troubles, he knew how wonderful and powerful God was. Still, what does that knowledge do for us when we can't see or sense God's nearness?

This is the tension of faith. Job believed God was the one he had worshiped up until his life was turned upside-down, but he couldn't see where God was in the midst of his pain. When we experience grief, we don't have to hide the tension. We can cry out for understanding and comfort while believing that God will come through.

Faithful One, when I can't see where you are or what you're doing, bolster my heart in courage.

Scripture Reading: Job 13-15

Courageous Faith

Though he slay me, I will hope in him;
yet I will argue my ways to his face.
Job 13:15 ESV

Job wasn't just going through a tough time. He was going through a crisis of faith. Still, it didn't cause him to back down from the Lord. God can handle our anger. He can handle our confusion. He isn't offended when we confront him with questions. We can argue our ways to his face, and he meets us with his powerful mercy.

It's easy to judge something we don't understand or haven't experienced. Isn't that what Job's friends were doing? They assumed he had sinned against God and this was his punishment. Yet, both God and Job knew the truth. Instead of judging people for what they go through, let's pray for God's mercy to meet them in their need.

Lord, thank you for the reminder that you can handle all of my big emotions. I bring them to you freely.

Scripture Reading: Job 16-18

Heavenly Advocate

Even now my witness is in heaven,
and my advocate is in the heights!
Job 16:19 CSB

We have a high priest who knows us well and advocates on our behalf, and his name is Jesus. He is our heavenly witness, and he lives to tell our story. He is the reason we can approach the throne of grace with confidence. There we find the grace and mercy to help us in our need (Hebrews 4:16).

No matter who speaks against you or misunderstands you, you can be confident that the truth of your circumstances is seen and testified to in the heavenly realm. Jesus is your advocate and help. Trust him to do what no one else can do. He has all you need, and your case is safe in his hands.

Jesus, thank you for being uncompromising in your understanding of the world and all that happens. You see me, know me, and advocate for me in my need, and I'm so grateful.

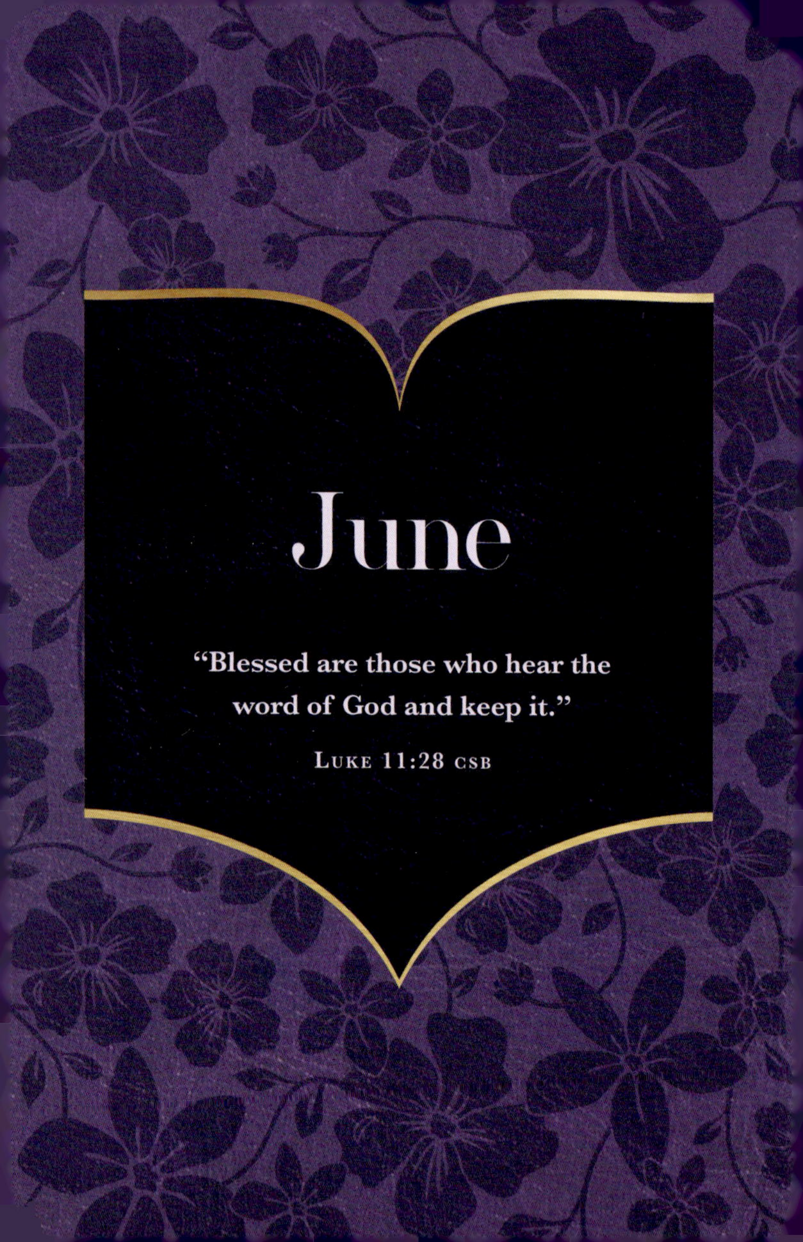
June
“Blessed are those who hear the
word of God and keep it.”
Luke 11:28 CSB

Scripture Reading: Job 19-21

My Redeemer Lives

Yet as for me, I know that my Redeemer lives,
And at the last, He will take His stand on the earth.
Even after my skin is destroyed,
Yet from my flesh I will see God,
Whom I, on my part, shall behold for myself,
And whom my eyes will see, and not another.
My heart faints within me!
JOB 19:25-27 NASB

There is no need to add to the faith-filled refrain of Job in today's verses. The truth and conviction of them stands as powerfully today as it did thousands of years ago. Let's join Job's statement of faith and make it our own.

No matter what has gone before or what comes after, our Redeemer lives. After we have breathed our last breath, he will be the face we see. We will truly live in the powerful life of our Redeemer and Savior at last!

Redeemer, my prayer is simple. You live, and I will see you. Thank you.

Scripture Reading: Job 22-24

Refining Fire

He knows the way that I take;
When He has tested me, I shall come forth as gold.
Job 23:10 NKJV

Just because we walk through trials does not mean we're being punished. Job wasn't being punished, though his faith was being tested. Each trial can serve to refine us when we submit ourselves in humility before the Lord.

James 1:2-3 serves as an encouragement in this regard. "Count it all joy when you fall into various trials, knowing that the testing of your faith produces patience." No one wants to suffer, but even suffering can yield beautiful results if we allow it to teach us. Let's hold on to the one who holds on to us even in the refining fire of hard times.

Refiner, I humble myself before you, and I ask you to bring beauty out of the ashes of disappointment, heartbreak, and suffering. I trust you.

Scripture Reading: Job 25-27

Faint Whispers

"These are only a small part of God's works.
We only hear a small whisper of him.
Who could understand God's thundering power?"
JOB 26:14 NCV

The most incredible things we know of God are only glimpses of his glorious might. Can you fathom that? The one who hung the stars in the sky and who put the mountains in their place is able to do far more than you can think or imagine.

If we're not humbled by the mighty power of God, we haven't yet understood how great he is! Though we cannot comprehend him, we get to know him more as he draws us to himself. This life is a journey of growing closer to him. One day, when we stand face-to-face with our King, we will know, and we will fall down in wonder.

Lord, thank you for your powerful mercy!

Scripture Reading: Job 28-30

Wisdom and Understanding

"The fear of the LORD —that is wisdom,
and to shun evil is understanding."
JOB 28:28 NIV

Wisdom is found by those who fear the Lord. They humble themselves before the mighty hand of God and follow his ways. The wisest thing we could do is trust the one who sees and knows all that we cannot comprehend.

Before we confuse fear with the need to be terrified of him, let's remember that it is God's kindness that leads us to repentance (Romans 2:4). God is merciful, and he is just. He is more powerful than we know. If we want wisdom and understanding, we will follow those longings straight to the Lord. By him all things were created, and he is the fullness of everything we could ever crave.

Mighty God, there is none like you. You see the big picture, but you don't miss the tiniest detail. Why would I not trust you with my life?

Scripture Reading: Job 31-33

God Is a Rescuer

God rescued me from the grave,
and now my life is filled with light.
Job 33:28 NLT

Elihu's motives weren't to tear Job down, though he did misunderstand him. There was truth sprinkled throughout his speech, and that can't be watered down. Sometimes, people will misunderstand us and appear to have the answers. They may even speak some truth, but it doesn't pertain to our situations. In those times, let's allow God to be our witness.

The truth is, God is a rescuer, and later we see that God rescues Job. Even when others misunderstand us, we can stand on the truth that God knows. He does what is right, and we can trust him to do it even when others can't understand our situation.

Lord, when others make assumptions and accusations based on their understanding rather than the truth, I will rest in your care. You right my wrongs.

Scripture Reading: Job 34-36

Unsearchable

Behold, God is great, and we know him not;
the number of his years is unsearchable.
JOB 36:26 ESV

God is greater than we know, but we are living in the age of revelation of who he is through Christ. We don't have to wonder what he is like. Jesus Christ, the Living Word, is the reflection of the Father, the living example of his character.

Yes, God is great. Yes, his ways are unsearchable, meaning he has no beginning or end. He is greater than the vastness of the skies, and his power goes beyond our ever-expanding universe. Still, if we want to know the Lord, to understand him better, we have a place to go. We have the person of Christ who gave his life for us. We have the Holy Spirit who teaches us the ways of God.

Lord Jesus, you revealed the nature of the Father, and you're still doing it today by the power of your testimony. Teach me, guide me, and make me more like you.

Scripture Reading: Job 37-39

God Speaks

"Where were you when I established the earth?
Tell me, if you have understanding."
Job 38:4 CSB

When God spoke, he didn't answer Job's questions, he established his great wisdom and power. God's perspective puts everything else in alignment. When we ask the Lord for answers, we might not get what we expect, but we will get what we need.

God is greater than we know. It's good for us to know our place and to know his. Sometimes we get too caught up in our problems that we think our lives are bigger than they are. Have you ever looked at a night sky or stood by an ocean and felt your tiny place in this world? That must be a little of what Job felt. Though we are small, God concerns himself with us. We can trust him to do what he has promised.

Lord, right my perspective in the truth of who you are and who I am in you. You are great, and I am small, but you take care of me.

Scripture Reading: Job 40-42

Transformed

I have heard of You by the hearing of the ear;
But now my eye sees You.
Job 42:5 NASB

Job had devoted his life to the Lord before he ever saw him. He based his faith on what he knew about him. But standing before the presence of God, he was forever transformed. What he knew about was now a personal experience that revolutionized his life.

Have you known about God but lack a personal encounter with his presence? In Matthew 28:20, Jesus promised to be with his followers even until the end of the age. That promise wasn't just for his disciples; it includes all who follow him, and that means you! If you have not been transformed by the love of God, now is the day to experience him.

Lord Jesus, I long to encounter the glory of who you are in a way that transforms me from the inside out. Shine on me, and open the eyes of my heart to see you.

Scripture Reading: Psalms 1-4

Strong Roots

He will be like a tree planted by streams of water,
Which yields its fruit in its season,
And its leaf does not wither.
PSALM 1:3 NKJV

When we meditate on God's Word, the roots of our faith grow down into the streams of living water. There we can grow in times of plenty or in want. The more we know God through his Word and through fellowship with his Spirit, the stronger our faith becomes.

There are simple ways to begin doing this, if it's not already a practice. We can memorize Scripture. We can sing songs based on God's Word (there are many). We can spend time in the morning and evening praying God's Word back to him. There is no wrong way to go about this, as long as the aim is to know the Lord.

God, I want to be like a tree planted by streams of living water. May my roots grow deep in your love!

Scripture Reading: Psalms 5-8

Daily Prayer

LORD, every morning you hear my voice.
Every morning, I tell you what I need,
and I wait for your answer.
PSALM 5:3 NCV

Daily devotion means daily connection with the Lord, and we do that through prayer. Every morning, offer God your heartfelt prayers. Ask him for what you need. You don't have to spend hours on your knees. Take your prayers on the go: while making your coffee, driving the kids to school, or in the quiet moments of the day.

When you begin your day in prayer, you set the tone of expectation. Let your waiting be active. Keep an open line of communication. As you do, pay attention to how God speaks, answers, and provides.

Lord, I want prayer to be more than a practice, I want it to be a natural extension of my relationship with you. Meet me in the morning, and throughout my day as I turn my heart toward you.

Scripture Reading: Psalms 9-12

Never Forsaken

The LORD is a refuge for the oppressed,
a stronghold in times of trouble.
Those who know your name trust in you,
for you, LORD, have never forsaken those who seek you.
PSALM 9:9-10 NIV

Those who trust in God and seek him are never forsaken. He is a safe place for those needing refuge. He is a strong tower in the time of trouble. Wherever you are today, know that you can run to the Lord and find the help you need.

Remember the testimonies that have come before of the Lord's faithfulness to answer. Draw upon your own experience with the Lord. Have hopeful expectation of his goodness in your present and future.

Refuge, I come running into the sacred rest of your presence. I need you. Surround me with songs of deliverance.

Scripture Reading: Psalms 13-16

Joyful Pleasure

You will show me the way of life,
granting me the joy of your presence
and the pleasures of living with you forever.
PSALM 16:11 NLT

When we follow the Lord, we don't simply have salvation for our souls (but let's rejoice in that truth). It's not just peace that is our portion (though his peace is great). The joy of the Lord becomes our great feast. As God reveals his life-giving ways, we share in the joy of his presence.

God is not a man that he would lie. He is not corrupt that he would lead us astray. He is better than the best of men, and he will continue to astound us with his powerful kindness as we know him more.

Lord, you have shown me the way of life, and I follow you. Bring me to deep wells of joy where my soul, heart, body, and mind come away refreshed in your love.

Scripture Reading: Psalms 17-20

A Spacious Place

He brought me out into a broad place;
he rescued me, because he delighted in me.
PSALM 18:19 ESV

Anxiety and stress can often feel like walls that are closing in on us. The pressure mounts, and we feel tighter. God's grace brings us out into the open. He releases the weight from our shoulders, takes us out of tight places, and gives us space to breathe, to roam, and to rest.

This was David's psalm of praise to the Lord on the day of his deliverance. We can take hope from his experience and rest on God's faithfulness to do the same for us. When we experience his delight, it is like a breath of fresh air to our lungs, clearing out the old and bringing joy, light, and favor.

God, release me from the tight places of stress I am under and lead me out into a spacious place.

Scripture Reading: Psalms 21-24

Good Shepherd

He renews my life;
he leads me along the right paths
for his name's sake.

Psalm 23:3 CSB

God is a good shepherd. He leads us beside still waters and restores our souls. He renews our lives, leading us along the paths he has set out. He does this all for the sake of his name. He is faithful, true, and good. He is powerful and just. He is merciful and gracious.

Sometimes, the path veers into darkness, and we cannot tell where we are going. That is when we can press closer to our good shepherd and trust his leadership. We have no reason to fear because our God keeps us safe. He fights our battles and protects our lives. We can trust him to do it!

Good Shepherd, lead me through the hills and valleys of life. I trust you to refresh, renew, and keep me all the days of my life. I am in your capable hand.

Scripture Reading: Psalms 25-28

What Confidence

The LORD is my light and my salvation;
Whom should I fear?
The LORD is the defense of my life;
Whom should I dread?
PSALM 27:1 NASB

When God is our light and salvation, why would we fear? It's a good reminder to place our hope in the all-powerful one. He is our salvation, our wisdom, and our strength. When he fights for us, no one can compete.

As Psalm 27 continues, we see David's true desire: not a good life with wealth, ease, or comfort, but a longing to know God. David wanted to experience the beauty of the Lord and to worship him in his holy place. He had caught a glimpse of God's goodness, and that was the foundation of his confidence.

Lord, you are my light and salvation. May every fear bow its knee at your name.

Scripture Reading: Psalms 29-32

In His Hand

As for me, I trust in You, O LORD;
I say, "You are my God."
My times are in Your hand.
PSALM 31:14-15 NKJV

When it's all said and done, it's good to know what our faith is based upon. Is it in what God can do for us, or is it based in who he is? None of us will live forever in these feeble human shells. Our souls will go on living, but these bodies fail.

This is not something to fear! God miraculously moves in our lives, and he will continue to, but he is not a fountain of youth. He is the eternal one. He is our God, and our times are in his hand. He knows how long we have, and we can trust him with it. May we trust God fully, not to escape death, but to come alive in his love.

Lord, you are the keeper of time, and I don't want to waste mine. Give me your perspective, and plant peace in my heart for this one, beautiful life you've given me to live.

Scripture Reading: Psalms 33-36

Loyal Love

LORD, your love reaches to the heavens,
your loyalty to the skies.
PSALM 36:5 NCV

God's faithful love reaches beyond the heavens. It cannot be contained, and we certainly can't exhaust it. Each day, we are met with abundant mercy. There is peace for our troubled hearts, grace for our weakness, and abundant love to cover every shame and fear.

Perfect love is too tall an order in our relationships with people. We try the best we can, but none of us gets it right all the time. Love covers offenses. Perfect love comes straight from the source of life. What others get wrong, God never misses. There isn't a wrong he can't right or an obstacle he can't overcome.

Lord, you are greater in love than any other. You don't pull back when I mess up. You press in further with compassion. I am in awe of you.

Scripture Reading: Psalms 37-40

Trust and Delight

Trust in the LORD and do good;
dwell in the land and enjoy safe pasture.
Take delight in the LORD,
and he will give you the desires of your heart.

PSALM 37:3-4 NIV

Trusting in the Lord with all our hearts, souls, minds, and strength looks like doing good. When we follow God's ways, we live in the wisdom, peace, and power of his mercy. We extend kindness and grace, and receive it just as readily. Perfection isn't the goal, goodness is.

The more we trust in the Lord, the more we delight in him. He is faithful and good. He is true and unwavering. Delighting in the Lord means that we don't drag our feet in following him or living out his love. When we've been transformed by his glorious mercy, the delight in doing good is all ours.

Lord, I trust you with every area of my life. I delight myself in you. As I draw closer to your goodness, I find not only my needs fulfilled, but my desires too.

Scripture Reading: Psalms 41-44

Direct Your Heart

Why am I discouraged?
Why is my heart so sad?
I will put my hope in God!
I will praise him again—
my Savior and my God!
PSALM 42:5-6 NLT

Life is hard, and some days we can't escape that reality. We don't have to pretend to not be feeling what we are in the moment. In our discouragement and sadness, we can still direct our hearts to the Lord in praise.

As we remind our hearts of the powerful faithfulness of God, our momentary troubles are put into perspective. God never changes. He will not fail to come through for us in our troubles. Let's feel what is present, what is real, and take that straight to our Savior today.

Lord, thank you for not turning away from me in my pain. When I feel discouraged, I will still turn my heart toward you in praise, for you are worthy.

Scripture Reading: Psalms 45-48

Present Help

God is in the midst of her; she shall not be moved;
God will help her when morning dawns.
PSALM 46:5 ESV

God has made his people his holy habitation. If you are in Christ, Christ is in you. You can be sure of his help, no matter what you face. If you find yourself in a position where you can't see the way out, trust your Savior. He has not abandoned you.

In your time of waiting, between your evident need and God's overt help, trust him. Let his presence be both your comfort and your confidence. You don't have to have the answer. Rely on your faithful God, and he will help you. Stand watch in prayer, and rest in his ability to do more than you can imagine.

Savior, thank you for the power of your love that meets me in my fear and makes me courageous. I rely on you for help.

Scripture Reading: Psalms 49-52

A Clean Heart

God, create a clean heart for me
and renew a steadfast spirit within me.
PSALM 51:10 CSB

It is never too late to turn away from our sins and come clean. The Lord meets us in our repentance and cleanses our hearts in pure love.

It is God's work to wash and renew us. His merciful sacrifice is what cleanses us, not anything we could do. We can't earn his love, and we can't lose it either. Every time we come to Christ with a humble heart, we are met with grace. We are met by mercy. We are cleansed, renewed, and set free.

Lord, create a clean heart for me and renew a steadfast spirit within me. I turn from my sins, and I receive the mercy of your love that cleanses me.

Scripture Reading: Psalms 53-56

Heartfelt Trust

When I am afraid,
I will put my trust in You.
PSALM 56:3 NASB

There's no question that you will feel fear in this life. The point isn't to escape it entirely. We cannot know what tomorrow will hold, but we can trust the one who does. Instead of trying to pretend we aren't afraid, let's take our real fear to the Lord. We need courage, and God knew that. There are hundreds of Scriptures where God tells us to not be afraid.

When we are afraid, it is what we do with that fear that either leads us further into a fear-based response or trust. Courage is pushing through the fear with faith. Let's follow the psalmist's lead and put our trust in God when we are afraid.

Savior, when I am afraid, I will put my trust in you. I will hope in you, for you are my help.

Scripture Reading: Psalms 57-60

Sing God's Goodness

As for me, I will sing of Your strength;
Yes, I will joyfully sing of Your faithfulness in the morning,
For You have been my refuge
And a place of refuge on the day of my distress.
PSALM 59:16 NKJV

Stir up your history with God and sing of what he's done for you. There's power in his faithfulness, and if you've been walking in his ways, you can be sure you've experienced it. There are many songs you could choose to sing: those written by psalmists, hymn writers, and modern-day songwriters. You could sing a spontaneous song of your own.

Whatever song you choose, sing out of the overflow of God's love. Give him your joyful song today, and connect to him through heartfelt worship.

God, you have been so good to me. I will sing of your love today.

Scripture Reading: Psalms 61-64

Deep Thirst

God, you are my God.
I search for you.
I thirst for you
like someone in a dry, empty land
where there is no water.
Psalm 63:1 NCV

Our deep soul longings for God will not go unmet. All who are thirsty will be filled, and all who hunger for righteousness will be satisfied in him.

Let your thirst lead you to the source of living water. Let your longings bring you before your Creator. Search for God, and you will find him. He is not far away, and he is not too busy to make time for you.

Lord, satisfy my longings in the living waters of your presence. Feed me with the nourishment of your Word. Meet me in my searching today.

Scripture Reading: Psalms 65-68

Burden Lifter

Praise be to the LORD, to God our Savior,
who daily bears our burdens.
PSALM 68:19 NIV

As long as it is called today, you have a God who lifts your burdens. Not only does he take the weight off your shoulders, but he carries it himself. Have too much on your plate and don't know how to handle it? Give it to the Lord, and he will help you do what needs to be done one step at a time without the overwhelming pressure of having to figure it out on your own.

Bring God the burdens you are carrying today, and trust him with them. He doesn't lose sight of a thing. You can't get rid of responsibilities, but you can transfer the pressure of them. Why suffer under the weight?

Lord, you are the lifter of my burdens and the strengthener of my hope. Thank you that I don't have to carry the weight of these things alone. Meet me in this place today.

Scripture Reading: Psalms 69-72

Constant Presence

O Lord, you alone are my hope.
I've trusted you, O Lord, from childhood.
Yes, you have been with me from birth.
Psalm 71:5-6 NLT

God is at work in the background of our lives before we realize he is there. Before we knew him, God knew and chose us. He is with us, waiting for us to turn to him. In his patience and thoughtful kindness, he has already put seeds of mercy in the soil of our lives.

When we come to the Lord, either for the first time or the hundredth, we can ask him to show us where he's been with us. He can alert us to the fingerprints of his kindness already on our lives. The one who faithfully brought us this far continues to go with us.

Faithful One, will you show me where you have been with me up until this point? I believe that you are constant. Bolster my faith in your faithfulness.

Scripture Reading: Psalms 73-76

Hope of the Hopeless

Let not the downtrodden turn back in shame;
let the poor and needy praise your name.
Psalm 74:21 ESV

God is near to the brokenhearted, and he takes care of the needy. It is always in line with his will when we pray for the vulnerable to be protected and the oppressed to be justified. The Lord sees every act of injustice, and he sees the needs of the destitute.

The hungry will be fed in God's kingdom. He never shuts his gates to those who need him. He lovingly welcomes all who come to him for help. Let's join God's heart and partner with his purposes by doing the same.

Lord, you are the hope of the hopeless. Help me to join with your heart and be a safe space and ready relief to those who need respite and care.

Scripture Reading: Psalms 77-80

Prayers for Restoration

Restore us, God;
make your face shine on us,
so that we may be saved.
PSALM 80:3 CSB

It is clear in this portion of the psalms that God's people went through some desperate times. They didn't ignore their humanity in the midst of it, freely pouring out their hearts before the Lord, but they did direct their prayers toward God's mercy.

God is the ultimate restorer. He can redeem what seems forever lost. He can put together what others dismantle in the powerful restoration of his mercy. Let's not lose hope when all seems lost. The darkest part of the night is right before the morning break. With the dawn comes relief. There is always a new day of mercy dawning.

Restorer, give me patience and perseverance in the moments of greatest pressure. I cry out to you for help.

Scripture Reading: Psalms 81-84

Open Wide

"I, the LORD, am your God,
Who brought you up from the land of Egypt;
Open your mouth wide and I will fill it."
PSALM 81:10 NASB

The God who delivered us is also the God who meets our needs. When he brought his people out of Egypt into the desert, they had nothing to eat, no gardens to pick from. What did God do? He sent manna from heaven—miraculously provided daily bread. He still provides for his people today.

If you are with God, there is nothing to fear. If you are drawing near to him and following his wisdom, there is no good thing he withholds from you! Take hope and take heart in his constant care. Press into his presence, for he does not only satisfy your physical needs, but your deepest emotional and spiritual needs too.

Lord, open the eyes of my heart that I may see, discern, and understand where you have been faithfully leading and providing for me.

Scripture Reading: Psalms 85-88

An Undivided Heart

Teach me Your way, O LORD;
I will walk in Your truth;
Unite my heart to fear Your name.
PSALM 86:11 NKJV

The Lord honors the prayers of his people. When we ask him to change our hearts, or to keep it whole and wholly devoted, his Spirit moves within us. We pair our willingness to learn with God's powerful wisdom, and we walk in his ways. As we do, we must continue to rely on him. He doesn't change even when we do.

An undivided heart is better than thinking we know more than we do. A heart of devotion and purpose puts God's kingdom above our own comfort. Let's put God first, follow his nudges toward consuming less of the world's ways, and put one foot in front of the other in loving action.

Lord, teach me your ways. As you show me what to do, help me to follow through.

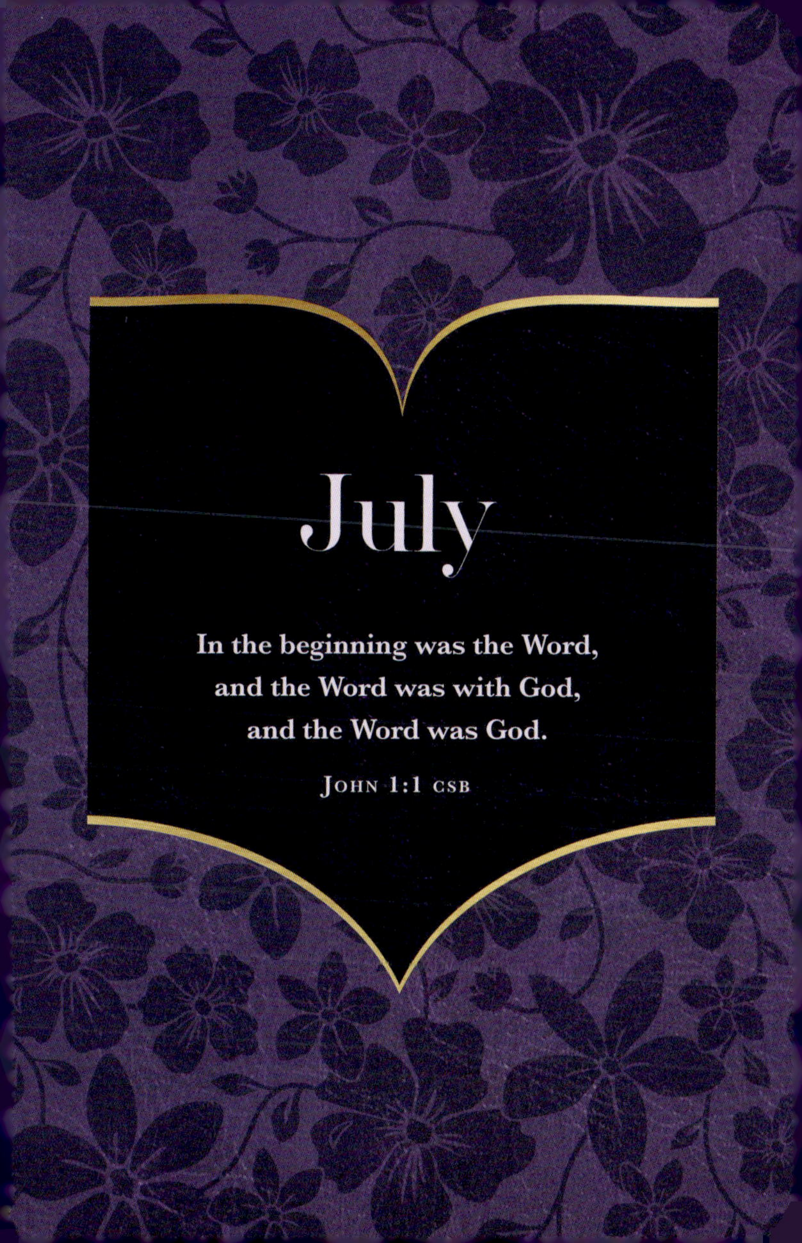
July
In the beginning was the Word,
and the Word was with God,
and the Word was God.
JOHN 1:1 CSB

Scripture Reading: Psalms 89-92

Fill Up

Fill us with your love every morning.
Then we will sing and rejoice all our lives.
PSALM 90:14 NCV

How we start our day matters. Have you ever slept through your alarm and had to rush to get to work? Or have you spent the first minutes of your day scrolling instead of easing into it with prayer and purpose? How did it affect the rest of your day?

We can learn to set the tone for our day. By beginning our day turning our attention to the Lord, we can bring peace to our mornings. We can fill up on the love of God which is just as necessary to our souls as breakfast is to our bodies. The more time we spend in God's presence simply to know him, the more rested, resourced, and ready we become for the rest of our day.

Lord, fill me up with your love every morning. You sustain and nourish me.

Scripture Reading: Psalms 93-96

Listen

He is our God
and we are the people of his pasture,
the flock under his care.
Psalm 95:7 NIV

The people of God are under his watchful care. We don't have to wonder whether he sees us in our joys or in our troubles. He sees all, understands all, and has wisdom to guide us through whatever we face.

His Word is our daily bread. Let's not depend on yesterday's bread to get us through. We need the life-giving energy of his Word today, and he freely offers it. If we listen for his voice, we will find the strength we need and the wisdom to follow his ways.

Lord, you are the God who hears, and you are the God who speaks. I listen for your living Word.

Scripture Reading: Psalms 97-100

Unfailing Goodness

For the LORD is good.
His unfailing love continues forever,
and his faithfulness continues to each generation.
PSALM 100:5 NLT

When we set our thoughts on the goodness of God, we will see even more of his kindness in the world around us. Meditating on God's love is never a waste of time. It fills us with the power of his mercy that sustains every living thing.

God's faithfulness continues to each generation. That means we are also recipients of his faithfulness. He hasn't turned away from us, and he hasn't abandoned us. Though the world is hard and heavy, and there are many wars and troubles, we have not driven God's love away. It is still present, it is still working, and his faithfulness continues.

Lord, I want to know the power of your goodness in good times and in hard. I want to know you more!

Scripture Reading: Psalms 101-104

Completely Removed

As far as the east is from the west,
So far does he remove our transgressions from us.
PSALM 103:12 ESV

When God forgives us, he completely removes the guilt of our sins. He doesn't hold our past against us. We may have a path of restoration to walk with those around us, but any hint of shame is gone in the presence of our Father's lovingkindness.

When we refuse to let ourselves walk in the liberty of God's love, we only hold ourselves back. The guilt, shame, and fear we lived in is no longer what defines us. Ask the Lord to show you the length of his love today and to give you a glimpse of his radical grace.

Lord, what you have forgiven, may I completely let go of. Remove forever the shadow of shame that I may be free.

Scripture Reading: Psalms 105-108

In Every Situation

Seek the LORD and his strength;
seek his face always.
PSALM 105:4 CSB

Instead of trying to prove ourselves, we can rely on the Lord and his strength in every situation we face. He is always wise, powerful, and true. When we partner our will with his, asking for heavenly insight, we become more productive in all we do.

There is never a situation where we can't seek God's face. There is never a reason to stay away. If we have set our hearts on the pilgrimage of following Christ, we have him always before us. It's never too late to start or to return to him.

Powerful One, I don't know why I try to prove myself to you. As I seek your perspective today, show me what you would do in the situations I'm in.

Scripture Reading: Psalms 109-112

Kind Father

You, God, the LORD, deal kindly with me
for the sake of Your name;
Because Your mercy is good, rescue me.
PSALM 109:21 NASB

God doesn't deliver us out of obligation. He delivers us out of the depths of his love. He is a good Father who cares about his children. We might picture him as an exasperated parent at the end of his proverbial rope, but he is better than the best of us. He is more patient, kind, and wise than we are.

This is the very best news. We don't have to doubt his love, but even if we do, he will prove faithful to his love, not to our expectation. God is endlessly kind to us, so why not turn to him over and over again?

Kind Father, I want to know you as you really are, not who I've been struggling to know you as. Transform my heart, my mind, and my expectations of your goodness.

Scripture Reading: Psalms 113-115

Divine Dignity

He raises the poor out of the dust,
And lifts the needy out of the ash heap,
That He may seat him with princes—
With the princes of His people.
PSALM 113:7-8 NKJV

We can tell a lot about a person based on how they talk about vulnerable people in society. Pride creates divisions between people while humility sees the inherent dignity within every person, no matter what they look like, where they come from, or what they lack.

God gives dignity to the least of us: the powerless, outcast, and poor. He always looks at the heart and judges from there, and he has compassion on all that he has made. Why would we think he wants us to do any differently? Let's give each other the dignity we have been created with, for we were all made in God's image.

Lord Jesus, you never called people names or shunned the people who came to you for help. You went to the weak, and you brought dignity to those society ignored. Help me to do the same.

Scripture Reading: Psalms 116-118

Joy for Today

This is the day that the LORD has made.
Let us rejoice and be glad today!
PSALM 118:24 NCV

Today is a fresh opportunity to experience the goodness of the Lord. This moment is the only time we can choose how we engage. Will we push off our praise until later or press in to know the Lord and worship him now?

The Lord is present in peace, and he is persistent in kindness. We have only to taste and see that he is good! Let's use this opportunity, before we move on to any other part of our day, and rejoice in him. Let's turn our gratitude toward him with hearts and lips that are overflowing with thanks.

Lord, I rejoice in your goodness today! You are worthy of my time and attention, so I pour out my heart to you today.

Scripture Reading: Psalm 119

Wise Devotion

Give me understanding, so that I may keep your law and obey it with all my heart.

Psalm 119:34 NIV

Understanding leads to devotion. The more we know the incomparable character of the Lord, the more convinced we become of his power, wisdom, and kindness. The more convinced we are of how wonderful he is, the more readily we follow him with wholehearted surrender.

It is wisdom that leads to the treasures of God's kingdom, and it is understanding that brings us to deep places of faith. When we ask the Lord for understanding, he will reveal himself in greater ways through his Spirit. He will give us the clarity of his wisdom, the power of his compassion, and the generosity of his grace.

Lord, I ask for greater understanding of the truth of who you are, so I don't hesitate in following after you.

Scripture Reading: Psalms 120-123

Higher Help

I look up to the mountains—
does my help come from there?
My help comes from the LORD,
who made heaven and earth!
PSALM 121:1-2 NLT

Even when you look to the hills and can't see physical help on its way to bail you out, you don't have to be discouraged. You aren't under siege in a closed-off valley, but even if you were, the Lord has a heavenly host ready to fight for you.

God himself watches over you. He stands beside you to protect you. God's help is present: it's present now, and it will be present in your future need. Don't give into worry when the God who created everything is your sun and shield!

Lord, you are my higher help. I lift my eyes up from the troubles that have been consuming me, and I set my heart on you.

Scripture Reading: Psalms 124-127

The Fruit Will Come

He who goes out weeping,
bearing the seed for sowing,
shall come home with shouts of joy,
bringing his sheaves with him.
PSALM 126:6 ESV

Every sorrowful season that you keep coming to the Lord, putting one foot in front of the other, no matter how slow or how small the movement may be, your harvest will reflect God's faithfulness to you.

Scripture assures us that sorrow may last for the night, but joy comes in the morning. We cannot always tell how long the night season goes on, or how long before seeding and reaping, but we can be sure that one follows the other. There is hope.

Lord, thank you for the assurance that sorrow won't last forever. I keep moving toward you and scattering the seed I have, and I trust that out of this season will come a fruitful harvest of joy.

Scripture Reading: Psalms 128-131

Abundant Redemption

Put your hope in the Lord.
For there is faithful love with the Lord,
and with him is redemption in abundance.
Psalm 130:7 CSB

There is no one too far gone from the mercy of God. There is no situation so awful that it can't be redeemed by God's power. Does that mean we have to stay close to them or stubbornly stick them out? Not unless God calls us to it. Not every mess is ours to clean up. We can't fix people. We can't control others' choices. We can only love them well, and sometimes we do that better from a distance.

Let's put our faith in God to do what only he can do, and trust him to do it. We can trust him with others, and we can trust him with us. He is faithful in love, powerful in salvation, and unlimited in gracious generosity.

Lord, thank you for the permission of your love. Show me whether you want me to press in or ease back.

Scripture Reading: Psalms 132-135

Pleasant Peace

Behold, how good and how pleasant it is
For brothers to live together in unity!
PSALM 133:1 NASB

It's a beautiful reflection of God's peace when we can dwell together in unity. If we spend our time arguing with each other, dividing walls go up. Love breaks down barriers. It creates pathways of peace because it prioritizes caring for each other over being right.

The need to be right isn't godly, and it's not humble. When we are open to each other, we are able to listen, not to know when we can speak, but to understand where the other is coming from. None of us is always meant to be the advice-giver, and none is always supposed to be the advice-receiver. It is give and take in the kingdom of Christ.

Lord, as far as I can, help me love others well so that I become a promoter of peace and unity.

Scripture Reading: Psalms 136-139

Wonderfully Made

I will praise You, for I am fearfully and wonderfully made;
Marvelous are Your works,
And that my soul knows very well.
PSALM 139:14 NKJV

You were made in the image of the Almighty God. You are his daughter, and he delights in who he created you to be. You don't have to become more than you are or diminish yourself before him to be accepted by his love. He loves you from an overflowing heart of love.

Know the marvelous beauty of God, not only in the world around you or in the evidence of his kindness in your life, but also in how he created you. He doesn't make mistakes. That doesn't mean you can't change your choices, hairstyle, or approach. But you don't have to do any of those things to be loved. You can't earn his love, and you certainly can't lose it.

Lord, when I look in the mirror, open my eyes to see the creativity and beauty you see.

Scripture Reading: Psalms 140-143

Present Portion

LORD, I cry out to you.
I say, "You are my protection.
You are all I want in this life."
PSALM 142:5 NCV

You don't have to wait another moment to know God as your portion. His Spirit is close. The Lord protects those who call on him for help, and the ones who hide themselves under his care can rest in peace.

What do you most need from God's Spirit today? Is it joy? Is it peace? Do you need a kind word, perspective, or wisdom? Do you need more hope? Whatever you need, God provides. Find all you need, and more than you know, in the presence of God.

Holy Spirit, even when I don't know exactly what I need, you do. Meet me with the portion I need as I come before you open to receive. I love you!

Scripture Reading: Psalms 144-147

Rich in Love

The LORD is gracious and compassionate,
slow to anger and rich in love.
The LORD is good to all;
he has compassion on all he has made.
PSALM 145:8-9 NIV

Psalm 145 reminds us of the nature of God. He is gracious. He is compassionate. He is slow to anger, and rich in love. These things always remain true, for God is the unchanging one. In Christ, there is forgiveness of sins, peace to settle our chaotic thoughts, and freedom to blossom into wholeness.

The Lord is good to all he has made, and he is compassionate to everyone who turns their face to him. Draw near to the light of his love today, and you will find yourself coming alive under the warmth of his gaze.

Lord, I draw near to you, laying down my misconceptions of who you are and what you must think of me.

Scripture Reading: Psalms 148-150

Praise the Lord

Let them all praise the name of the LORD.
For his name is very great;
his glory towers over the earth and heaven!
PSALM 148:13 NLT

The psalms close out with chapters instructing all who hear to praise the Lord! Let's take the cue, and offer God our uninhibited praise today. He is the God who created us, who shows us infinite love, and who never leaves us.

There are so many reasons to praise him in the truth of his powerful being. What reasons can you think of today? From the simple and seemingly silly to the overwhelmingly good reasons you find, offer them all to him in praise, for he loves to delight in you when you turn toward him.

Lord, I praise you, not because I have to, but because I get to! You have been wonderful to me.

Scripture Reading: Proverbs 1-3

Wholehearted Trust

Trust in the LORD with all your heart,
and do not lean on your own understanding.
In all your ways acknowledge him,
and he will make straight your paths.

PROVERBS 3:5-6 ESV

When we question our way, this verse is a powerful foundation to come back to and stand upon. If we trust the Lord wholeheartedly, even when we cannot understand what he is doing, and follow him, he straightens the path before us.

We acknowledge the Lord as we go, welcoming in his leadership as we do. That doesn't mean we stand still until we can see far down the path. As we move, he directs us, and he reveals each step as we go.

Lord, trust is needed in this life, and it almost always feels vulnerable. I trust you will guide and redirect me when necessary.

Scripture Reading: Proverbs 4-6

Moments of Correction

A command is a lamp, teaching is a light,
and corrective discipline is the way to life.
PROVERBS 6:23 CSB

The Lord leads us in his way, but he knows we will not follow him perfectly. Part of learning and practicing walking in the way of God's kingdom is knowing we will not get it right every time. It shouldn't surprise us when this happens, and we don't have to feel ashamed. When God corrects us, it is done in kindness. He lovingly leads us back to the heart of his truth, and we can learn from mistakes made.

Pride keeps us from change. A humble heart is ready to receive, correct its course, and do things differently. God knows us through and through; he doesn't expect more than we can offer.

Lord, I don't want to resist your correction as if you expected me to get it all right. Teach me your better way.

Scripture Reading: Proverbs 7-9

Source of Life

Anyone who listens to me is happy,
watching at my doors every day,
waiting by the posts of my doorway.
For the one who finds me finds life
and obtains favor from the LORD.

PROVERBS 8:34-35 NASB

God is not only the source of our breath, beating hearts, and existence; he is the source of every good and perfect gift. Everything that is life-giving is found in him. We don't have to go searching for meaning in others. We will find it as we keep our hearts connected to the source of life itself.

We can actively listen, watch, and wait for the Lord as we go about our day: at work, with our family and friends, and while engaged in hobbies. It is a posture of the heart, and it can be done anywhere.

Lord, you are the source of all life. I open my heart to listen, watch, and wait for you as I move through my day.

Scripture Reading: Proverbs 10-12

Generous Soul

The generous soul will be made rich,
And he who waters will also be watered himself.
PROVERBS 11:25 NKJV

Generosity is a fruit of wisdom. God, who doesn't withhold from those who ask him for help, calls us to grow in our ability to share freely with others. If we treat our resources like the gifts they are, we will gladly spread practical kindness by walking in the generosity of Christ.

Jesus warned that it is hard for the rich to enter the kingdom. Why? Not because it's impossible, but because there is a lot to sacrifice. Whether we have a little or a lot, it is important that we grow in generosity. As we practice choosing generosity, we will experience the power of it as gratitude wells up within.

Generous One, you are so rich in love. You are not stingy, and I don't want to be either. Help me grow in generosity as I make efforts to share what I have.

Scripture Reading: Proverbs 13-15

Wise Friends

Spend time with the wise and you will become wise,
but the friends of fools will suffer.
PROVERBS 13:20 NCV

According to Scripture, wisdom is seen in generosity, compassion, patience, honesty, and thoughtful action. If we want to become wise, the first step toward wisdom is to surround ourselves with those who embody wisdom.

Wisdom is found in the fruit of a life, not just in what a person says or in the power they wield over others. Wisdom is found in gentle responses in a highly pressurized moment. It is found in taking time rather than rushing into a decision without regard for the consequences.

Lord, I want to grow in your wisdom. Show me which relationships to press into and which to ease back from, with the fruit of those lives as my guide.

Scripture Reading: Proverbs 16-18

Gracious Words

Gracious words are a honeycomb,
sweet to the soul and healing to the bones.
PROVERBS 16:24 NIV

How we speak to others matters. Considering our words and their effects is an act of wisdom. We've all been in the company of less than gracious people. The effects of their words can be long-lasting. Instead of building us up, they break us down.

Gracious words are a honeycomb. They feel like a balm to the soul, sweet and healing as they sink in. What a beautiful gift they are. Gracious words are not insincere. They are based in truth, love, and wisdom. They offer compassion, kindness, and clarity. A gracious response is a gift.

Gracious God, I want to be someone who offers kindness, consideration, and grace when I speak to others. Help me to grow in this area.

Scripture Reading: Proverbs 19-21

Prevailing Purpose

You can make many plans,
but the LORD's purpose will prevail.
PROVERBS 19:21 NLT

God doesn't discourage us from making plans. But when it all comes down to it, we can take a deep sigh of relief. His purposes are not dependent on our plans. He is faithful to his Word and his nature. What he has promised, he will do—with or without us.

We were not created to be workhorses for the Lord. He created us out of love to walk with him. He loves for us to know him, and he longs to reveal how well he knows us. We were created for relationship first. Everything else is extra!

Powerful God, I want to know the deep relief of trusting you fully. From that place, I can live in the liberty of your love all my days, including this very day.

Scripture Reading: Proverbs 22-24

Good Character

A good name is to be chosen rather than great riches,
and favor is better than silver or gold.
PROVERBS 22:1 ESV

If we work on our character rather than what might impress others, we invest in the most precious thing we have. A good character is better than wealth. Trustworthy people are worth more than silver or gold.

We are all in process, but hopefully we are in the process of refinement, becoming more like God with each day. It's never too late to choose differently. If we want to walk in wisdom, today is a perfect day to begin. When we speak the truth in love, encourage those who need it, and choose integrity, others will take notice.

Lord, more than anything, may my character be beautiful and reflective of you.

Scripture Reading: Proverbs 25-27

Reflections

As water reflects the face,
so the heart reflects the person.
PROVERBS 27:19 CSB

Our hearts reflect who we are. The good news is that we're not static beings. We can grow, change, and make different choices. If we find ourselves in need of a heart change, God is near and ready to move. He is the one who melts the icy edges. He is able to renew, restore, and transform us from the inside out.

Before we jump to conclusions about who we are or aren't, let's go to the Lord for a fresh perspective. Let's ask him to speak over our hearts and minds to reveal what he sees. What we may miss with a critical eye, he sees in fullness. We can trust his kindness and his power.

Lord, thank you for the reminder that you can change what no one else can.

Scripture Reading: Proverbs 28-29

Refuge of Trust

Fear of man will prove to be a snare,
but whoever trusts in the LORD is kept safe.
PROVERBS 29:25 NIV

When we allow the fear of what others think to dictate our actions, it always ends up being a trap. It is better to trust the Lord than to fear others. Even the most powerful people cannot avoid God's gaze.

Let's align our hearts in trust, and follow the ways of Christ. His love is unfailing, and his grace is near. He will guide us through even the most treacherous storms of this life with peace as our portion and his confident care as our courage.

Unfailing One, I don't want to let fear of others keep me from walking in freedom. I choose you.

Scripture Reading: Proverbs 30-31

Honorable Fruit

Charm is deceptive, and beauty does not last;
but a woman who fears the LORD will be greatly praised.
PROVERBS 31:30 NLT

Charm and beauty can open doors for us in the short-term, but they mean nothing without the strength of character built on integrity.

As we age, our relationship to our bodies change, and the shift can be incredibly liberating. It's not wrong to want to look nice. But let's not spend so much time on our exterior that we miss out on building the best beauty routine possible—a willing, humble heart before the Lord. As we clothe ourselves in his love and follow his ways, the sweet fruit of his presence follows us.

Lord, I want to reveal the power of your goodness in my life, and it begins in my heart. You can have it!

Scripture Reading: Ecclesiastes 1-4

The Process of Becoming

For everything there is a season, and a time for every matter under heaven. He has made everything beautiful in its time.

ECCLESIASTES 3:1,11 ESV

Not every season of this life is beautiful. Still, we have the promise of God in both hard times and good that he is near, and he makes all things beautiful in their time. This includes each of us! We will bloom as his love takes root in our hearts, and nothing will be wasted.

We might feel the pangs of growth, but that means we're alive, and God is doing his work. Let's trust God in every season. We cannot rush the cycles, but we can trust God to be with us in every one. He is making our lives beautiful.

Beautiful Lord, let the fragrance of your goodness be found in my life, no matter the season or my state in it.

Scripture Reading: Ecclesiastes 5-8

Don't Give Up

The end of a matter is better than its beginning;
a patient spirit is better than a proud spirit.
ECCLESIASTES 7:8 CSB

Patience is better than pride. Pride demands answers without trust. It doubles down on what it knows rather than being curious about what it doesn't. When we don't have answers, it's not the time to pretend we do. This is when we can lean into trust and practice patience in the space between question and answer.

There is so much we do not, and cannot, know in this life. But we know the one who sees it all, who created us from dust. We catch glimpses of his goodness, of the arc of his love, as we lean on him. One day we will see it fully, just as we are fully seen and known.

Lord, lead me in your capable wisdom and meet me in the vulnerability of trust.

Scripture Reading: Ecclesiastes 9-12

Strength for Today

Whatever your hand finds to do, do it with all your might.
ECCLESIASTES 9:10 NASB

We cannot change what we did yesterday, and we can't imagine ourselves into the future. Today is all we're given. It is all we can do anything with. Why, then, would we put off the good we can do today?

God gives us strength for each day. He knows what we will face before we do, and he offers us the power of his presence to empower us for each challenge. Let's be dedicated in our work, doing what is ours to do today. What is on your plate today? What is important? It might change from day to day, but the Lord doesn't. He gives you strength for whatever it is. Go to him first, and then bring him with you into all you do.

Lord, your presence is my strength. Bless the work of my hands and the relationships I tend to.

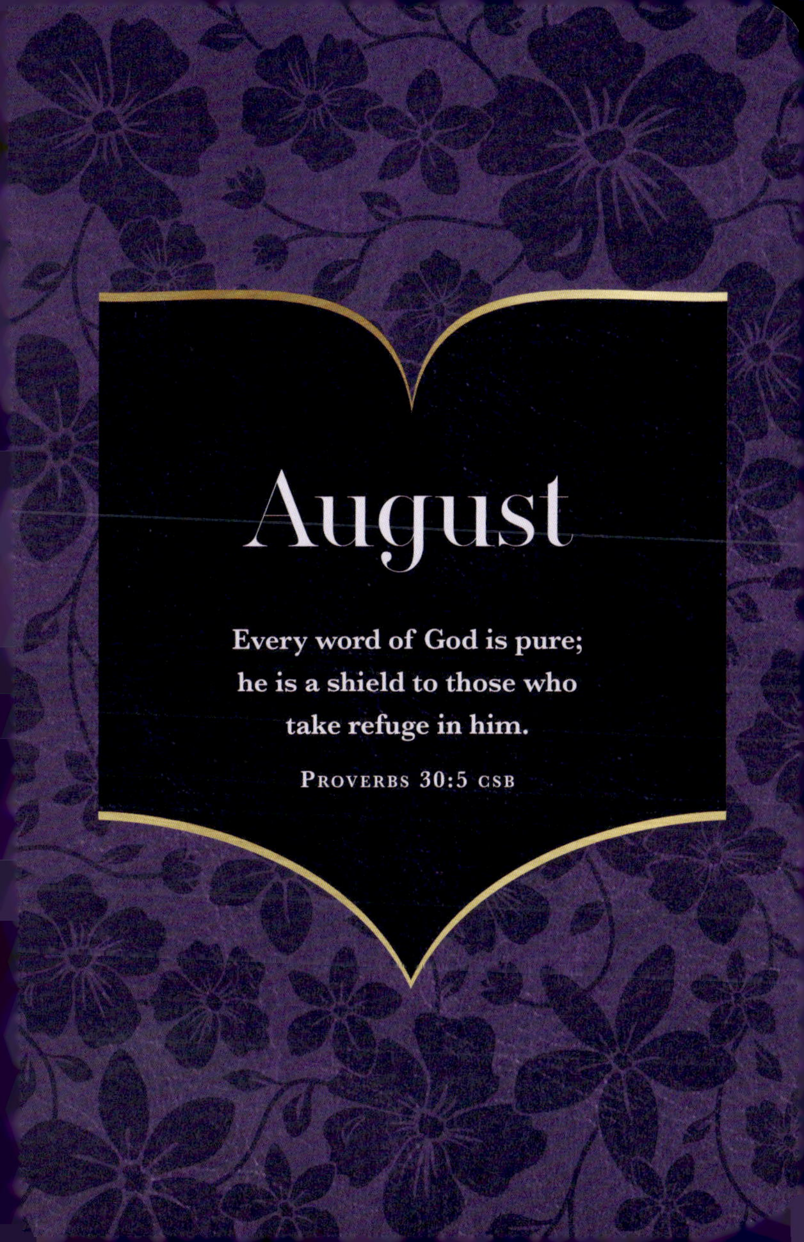
August
Every word of God is pure;
he is a shield to those who
take refuge in him.
Proverbs 30:5 CSB

Scripture Reading: Song of Solomon 1-4

Invitation

"Rise up, my love, my fair one,
And come away.
For lo, the winter is past…
The time of singing has come."
SONG OF SOLOMON 2:10-12 NKJV

The winter is past, and the time of singing has come. Take God's loving hand and rise up to meet him. He is leading you out of the dark winter into the newness of life in a springtime for your soul. Where there was barrenness, there is new life blooming. Can you sense it?

God is calling you to leave the cocoon of your comfort and to follow him into the wilds of his love. You can trust his heart. He will not lead you to harm. He is faithful, true, merciful, and just. He never fails in lovingkindness. Will you rise up and come away with him?

Lord, I don't want to stay anywhere longer than you have for me: physically, emotionally, or otherwise. I will follow you.

Scripture Reading: Song of Solomon 5-8

Beloved

I am my beloved's and my beloved is mine.
SONG OF SOLOMON 6:3 NIV

Relationship with God isn't a one-way street. You are not sending up your prayers to a phone line in the sky, hoping someone will pick up and hear you. You are also not alone in your desire for God. God placed desire in your heart, but his burns even brighter than you know.

You were meant to know God not just with your head, but also with your heart. He is yours, and you are his. The more you know him, the more you will love him. The more you love him, the more you will see his love for you. There is no limit to the closeness you can have with him. He loves to meet you in the mundane and bring beauty out of the ordinary.

Lord, I want to know you more, to know with certainty that I am beloved to you. May I know with even greater certainty that you are also mine.

Scripture Reading: Isaiah 1-4

White as Snow

"Though your sins are like scarlet,
I will make them as white as snow.
Though they are red like crimson,
I will make them as white as wool."

Isaiah 1:18 NLT

God is able to make all things new. His redemption power can purify and cleanse our guilt and make us white as snow. He removes shame, fear, sin, and death. He replaces it with grace as we come to him with repentant hearts. He transforms us from the inside out, and our lives shine brighter.

Where there is healing, there is hope. Where there is redemption, there is a miracle of mercy. God does what no one else can, and we can trust him to do it for each of us who comes before him in spirit and in truth.

Redeemer, you have taken my sin and shame and wiped the stain of it away in your redemptive love. Thank you!

Scripture Reading: Isaiah 5-8

Heard and Answered

I heard the voice of the LORD saying, "Whom shall I send, and who will go for us?" Then I said, "Here I am! Send me."

ISAIAH 6:8 ESV

God hears us and answers us, but how often do we listen for him? Isaiah overhead the Lord, and instead of waiting for God to call him, he volunteered himself for the task. If we have any desire in our hearts to serve God after seeing a need, we don't have to doubt whether it will honor him or not.

Come before the Lord with your desire to serve him, and ask him to anoint you for the task. Let your willingness be the catalyst that calls you.

Lord, when I feel compelled to serve in love, I will bring it to you.

Scripture Reading: Isaiah 9-12

Great Light

The people walking in darkness
have seen a great light;
a light has dawned
on those living in the land of darkness.
Isaiah 9:2 csb

This portion of Isaiah is a prophecy of the coming Messiah. When Jesus Christ came, he was the way, the truth, and the life. He was the light of life that shone for all to see. The radiant favor of God rose on the dawning of his life, and it has not set.

We are living in the light of Christ still today. Be encouraged. Draw near to him, and he will draw near to you. Every fear flees in his presence, and every heart is set to rest in his confident kindness. Stand in the light of your Savior today.

Savior, you are the light of the world, and you shine on me today. You are my hope, my freedom, and my peace.

Scripture Reading: Isaiah 13-16

Sure Plans

"Certainly, just as I have intended, so it has happened, and just as I have planned, so it will stand."
ISAIAH 14:24 NASB

We make the best plans we can with the resources and information we have, but even our best-laid plans don't account for unseen challenges. God's plans take everything we cannot see or know into account. We might be discouraged by setbacks, but God is never surprised.

God's promises are yes and amen. What he sets into motion, no one can undo. What he vows to do, he faithfully follows through on. It might not be in our time, or the way we imagine, but that doesn't mean that he has failed. Let us put our wholehearted trust in the one who sees the end from the beginning and everything in-between.

Lord, when I am discouraged because of the challenges of life, shift my perspective to your faithfulness.

Scripture Reading: Isaiah 17-20

Look to Your Maker

In that day a man will look to his Maker,
And his eyes will have respect for the Holy One of Israel.
Isaiah 17:7 NKJV

It is always the right time to look to your Maker. You don't have to wait for a day of trouble or when everything calms down. This is the day to turn your heart toward him in humble surrender.

When you set your eyes on your Maker, remember who he is. He is the source of all life, including your own. You wouldn't be here without him, and his lovingkindness draws you to his heart today. He is trustworthy and true, and he can help you through anything. He loves to meet you in the little things as well as the big.

Holy One, you are worthy of my surrender, my attention, and my praise. I turn to you today with a heart that honors you.

Scripture Reading: Isaiah 21-24

Songs of Praise

We hear songs from every part of the earth
praising God, the Righteous One.
ISAIAH 24:16 NCV

Even when there is so much evil happening in the world, there are still songs of praise going up to the God who is faithful and true. He rescues those who turn to him, and he redeems those who had no other hope. Let's join our songs of praise with worshiping believers from around the world.

There is nowhere in this earth where God's Spirit is absent. We couldn't run away from him if we tried (Psalm 139). This is exceedingly good news, for the God who pursues our hearts is as close as our breath when we turn to him. We don't have to walk to the ends of the earth to find him. A whispered song of praise is enough to get his attention.

Righteous One, I will praise you when I'm on the mountaintops of life, and I will praise you in the valleys. I will sing to you, for you are worthy.

Scripture Reading: Isaiah 25-28

Perfect Peace

You will keep in perfect peace
those whose minds are steadfast,
because they trust in you.
Trust in the LORD forever,
for the LORD, the LORD himself, is the Rock eternal.
ISAIAH 26:3-4 NIV

A steadfast mind is one that has unwavering trust in the Lord. It doesn't mean that every thought will reflect that. Thoughts come from various influences, and we get to choose which ones to believe.

Perfect peace is a gift from God as we turn our attention to him. We offer him our thoughts, and he settles them. No matter the day or the hour, we can trust the Lord.

Lord, you are my peace. I turn my mind toward you in unwavering trust. No matter what anxieties come up, you are the Prince of Peace.

Scripture Reading: Isaiah 29-32

Personal Leadership

Your own ears will hear him.
Right behind you a voice will say,
"This is the way you should go,"
whether to the right or to the left.
ISAIAH 30:21 NLT

The blessings of God's people include his love and compassion for those who wait for him. He is gracious when they ask for help. He is a ready teacher for those who look to him. He reveals himself to searching hearts by directing them with his wisdom.

Have you ever had a personal experience of being led by the Lord? It doesn't matter how long or how short you've been walking with him; you can know his leadership. He loves to direct his people. Wait on him, and you will know the personal power of his leadership.

God, you are my Savior and my help, but you are also my loving leader. I want to know your voice and follow it.

Scripture Reading: Isaiah 33-36

Daily Strength

O LORD, be gracious to us; we wait for you.
Be our arm every morning,
our salvation in the time of trouble.
ISAIAH 33:2 ESV

In times of need, it is natural to turn to the Lord for strength. If we build practices of connection, it doesn't matter what we're going through; our hearts search for him each morning, and he meets us with grace.

It is good to have a habit of prayer first thing every morning. It sets the tone for the rest day. As we ask him to meet us with the strength of his presence, we will be met. Just as we need daily bread to sustain our bodies, we need the daily bread of his Word and the power of his fellowship to feed our souls, hearts, and minds.

O Lord, you are my daily bread. Feed me with the nourishment of your Word. Satisfy my thirst with the waters of your Spirit.

Scripture Reading: Isaiah 37-40

Ease in the Effort

Those who trust in the LORD
will renew their strength;
they will soar on wings like eagles;
they will run and not become weary,
they will walk and not faint.
ISAIAH 40:31 CSB

Life doesn't magically become effortless when we put our trust in the Lord, but it does become easier. We still put the effort in: we need to keep going, to walk, to run, to sometimes soar. It's in Christ that our strength is renewed and we have the energy and resources to persevere.

God gives strength to the faint and powerless. It is exactly in those moments of great need that God renews us. Let's not be discouraged when we're tired and powerless. Those are the moments of our greatest breakthrough.

Lord, you bring greater ease to the efforts of life. Thank you for your strength and your nearness.

Scripture Reading: Isaiah 41-44

Fully Engaged

"Do not call to mind the former things,
Or consider things of the past.
Behold, I am going to do something new,
Now it will spring up;"

Isaiah 43:18-19 NASB

The past can be a place of learning, but if we're constantly reaching for what is behind us, we can't live in the power of the present or the hope of the future. God doesn't want us to be so fixated on what is behind that we miss out on all the goodness he has in store for us.

God is always doing something new. No two sunsets are the same. He creates glorious connections each and every day. If we will but open our eyes and look for the marks of his mercy, we will find them.

Merciful God, I don't want to be stuck in the past. I don't want to miss out on the beauty of the now. Open my eyes to what you are doing.

Scripture Reading: Isaiah 45-48

Ageless Love

"Even to your old age, I am He,
And even to gray hairs I will carry you!
I have made, and I will bear;
Even I will carry, and will deliver you."
ISAIAH 46:4 NKJV

You cannot age out of God's care. Once his daughter, always his daughter. He delights in you all the days of your life. Why not embrace his wonderful love and believe him when he promises that he will be with you wherever you go? Though you might feel the shift in other's reception of you, God will never forget you. He won't overlook you. You matter to him always.

You can know the power of his grace as he breathes fresh hope and vision on your life. He's not done with you. You have so much life left to live, and though it might look different than it did in your youth, it is no less worthwhile or beautiful.

Father, thank you for your persistent and tender care of me. Breathe fresh hope into my soul as you reveal your love to me in deeper ways.

Scripture Reading: Isaiah 49-52

Behind and Before

The LORD will go before you,
and the God of Israel will guard you from behind.
ISAIAH 52:12 NCV

Not only does God go before you in your circumstances, he also closes you in from behind. He has got you covered, so you don't need to worry. God is your wraparound shield in every battle, and he is your steady hand of guidance on rugged paths.

You can trust the Lord with your days. He knows the number of them already, and he will guide you in goodness as you look to him. Submit yourself to him, and trust him to bring you to where you need to be at the right time.

Lord, you are the God who goes before and behind me, and I trust you to keep me all the days of my life. You are my courage and my confidence.

Scripture Reading: Isaiah 53-56

Unshakable Foundations

"Though the mountains be shaken
and the hills be removed,
yet my unfailing love for you will not be shaken
nor my covenant of peace be removed,"
says the LORD, who has compassion on you.

ISAIAH 54:10 NIV

When everything feels as though it's falling apart, take heart! There is a foundation that remains sturdy beneath the feet of those who rely on the Lord. His unfailing love will never leave, never crumble. It is sure and strong.

God's covenants cannot be revoked. His love and peace are always available to those who remain in covenant with him. We are met with grace and compassion every time we turn to him.

Father, you are gracious and compassionate, and you are my firm foundation. I stand on you.

Scripture Reading: Isaiah 57-60

True Fasting

"No, this is the kind of fasting I want:
Free those who are wrongly imprisoned;
lighten the burden of those who work for you.
Let the oppressed go free,
and remove the chains that bind people."

ISAIAH 58:6 NLT

True fasting isn't about going without, it's about being generous with what we have. What God really wants is our devoted worship. When we partner with his purposes, we advocate for justice for the vulnerable and wrongly accused, and we lighten the loads of the burdened.

God wants us to reflect him. His nature is merciful, just, and true. He delights in truth. Let's let our lives speak for our spirituality, not the outer religious practices that may or may not reflect a devoted heart.

Lord, I want to worship you in spirit and in truth. May my life, my choices, and my service reflect who you are.

Scripture Reading: Isaiah 61-63

Abundance of Love

I will recount the steadfast love of the LORD,
the praises of the LORD…
according to the abundance of his steadfast love.
ISAIAH 63:7 ESV

It is good to remember what the Lord has done before. We can use history with God's faithfulness to encourage our hearts in worship today. What God has done before, he can do again. He is steadfast; his loving nature never shifts! He is always overflowing in it.

It is not too much to remember his love every day. Our hearts need the reminder. We are loved, and it is from that place of kindness, mercy, and compassion that we can do all things through Christ who gives us strength.

Lord, may I never grow weary of your love. It is the lifeforce of my heart, soul, and body. It is the strength that empowers me to walk with you in wisdom, humility, and joy.

Scripture Reading: Isaiah 64-66

Molded

Lord, you are our Father;
we are the clay, and you are our potter;
we all are the work of your hands.
Isaiah 64:8 csb

We are the work of the Father's hands. He is the potter who molds us for his good pleasure, and we are the clay. There is nothing in our natural bodies that offends him. He knows us intricately, and he made us as we are.

Do you ever wonder why God made you the way he did? Ask him! Look in a mirror today, and try to see yourself through the eyes of your Creator. Join with his heart of love and learn to love the parts of you that you've struggled to like. God delights in who you are, and he is continuing to mold you into his image.

Father, thank you for this body, this mind, this heart. I am made in your image and yet wholly unique.

Scripture Reading: Jeremiah 1-4

Known and Consecrated

"Before I formed you in the womb I knew you,
And before you were born I consecrated you."
JEREMIAH 1:5 NASB

Even before God formed you, he knew you. He knew who he would create you to be. Not only that, but he consecrated you for the life and work you have been called to do! You don't have to earn his attention or favor. You already have it as his beloved daughter.

Do you live in the power of this perspective? Have you yielded your heart to the one who knows you best? There isn't a hill he can't level or bring you to the top of as you rely on him. He already knows the trajectory of your life, and you get to partner with him as you make the choice to follow his ways. You can't mess it up, for his grace goes with you always.

Lord, you are the one who knows me best, and I want to give you my best. Prepare my hands for what you've prepared for me to do, and lead me on the path of life that honors you most.

Scripture Reading: Jeremiah 5-8

Ancient Paths

"Stand in the ways and see,
And ask for the old paths, where the good way is,
And walk in it;
Then you will find rest for your souls."

JEREMIAH 6:16 NKJV

You don't have to know how to move ahead to ask for wisdom. You could have lived your life one way up to this point and decide you want something different. If you go asking for the ancient paths of wisdom, God will lead you on the pathway of his peace.

If you long for peace, you can find it today. As you walk in the good way of Christ, you will find rest for your soul and powerful peace for your portion. The ancient paths are built upon the foundations of God's kingdom and his very nature. Though he is a mystery, his ways are clear. Walk in them.

Ancient One, your ways are the ancient paths. I choose to trust your wisdom and mercy and walk in your good way.

Scripture Reading: Jeremiah 9-12

Righteous One

"If people want to brag, let them brag
that they understand and know me.
Let them brag that I am the Lord,
and that I am kind and fair,
and that I do things that are right on earth."

Jeremiah 9:24 ncv

God's words here are astounding. If we want to brag about God, it is not about his power, his judgment, or his perfect nature that we should boast about. If we truly know his nature, we know what matters most to him. He is kind, fair, and righteous. He does what is right on the earth.

There are many who boast about the judgment of God as if it were something to delight in. But God delights in showing mercy, compassion, and grace. He is close to the vulnerable and broken. He delights in redemption and restoration. He makes wrong things right.

Lord, when I talk about you to others, may it reflect who you say you are—kind, fair, and righteous.

Scripture Reading: Jeremiah 13-16

Not Forsaken

You are among us, LORD,
and we bear your name;
do not forsake us!
JEREMIAH 14:9 NIV

The Lord doesn't forsake his people. We can pray with boldness before him when it feels as if he's far away. It's reminiscent of Psalm 38:21, where David prayed, "Lord, do not forsake me; do not be far from me, my God."

When we need reassurance, let's turn both to his presence and his living Word. James 4:8 promises, "Come near to God, and he will come near to you." Hebrews 4:16 says, "Let us then approach God's throne of grace with confidence, so that we may receive mercy and grace to help us in our time of need." With boldness, let's approach God and call on his name. He will faithfully meet us.

Lord, you never forsake those who trust in you. I rely on you, God, and I will boldly come before your throne of grace whenever I need you.

Scripture Reading: Jeremiah 17-20

Thriving Roots

"Those who trust in the LORD …
are like trees planted along a riverbank,
with roots that reach deep into the water.
Such trees are not bothered by the heat
or worried by long months of drought.
Their leaves stay green,
and they never stop producing fruit."

JEREMIAH 17:7-8 NLT

Putting our trust in God, our Savior, is the safest and surest bet in this life. All who plant their roots in him are fed. He doesn't give us just enough to keep us alive, but he is the true life source that makes us thrive.

It is in harsh times when those who are planted by the streams of living water shine brightest. The fruit of the Spirit is still evident. When we are fed by the Spirit, we produce the fruit of the Spirit.

Holy Spirit, thank you for the power of your presence that sustains me.

Scripture Reading: Jeremiah 21-24

For Our Good

"I will set my eyes on them for good, and I will bring them back to this land. I will build them up, and not tear them down; I will plant them, and not pluck them up."

JEREMIAH 24:6 ESV

It can be difficult to turn our hearts toward the Lord in trust. The little good we can do on our own is honored by him, and he blesses us with his incomparable goodness. He builds up those who come to him in humble surrender.

Jesus Christ is our Redeemer, and that will always be true. He gives grace upon grace to those who come to him. When we hold back from him, we are the ones who miss out, not him. Though he loves us and passionately pursues us, we must be the ones who turn to him.

Redeemer, you are my hope, and in you I find my strength.

Scripture Reading: Jeremiah 25-28

Corrective Choices

Correct your ways and deeds, and obey the LORD your God so that he might relent concerning the disaster he had pronounced against you.

JEREMIAH 26:13 CSB

God does not delight in suffering. He longs to redeem not destroy. He responds with mercy every time we turn to him. When we make the choice to change our ways, and we ask for his help to do it, he rushes in with gracious strength to empower us.

God transforms hearts, but he also requires our participation. He doesn't force his will or ways on anyone. He invites us to his kingdom, but we have to take him up on the invitation. It's never too late to make a different choice.

Lord, I recognize I have choices to make in my life. I turn toward you and ask for your help.

Scripture Reading: Jeremiah 29-32

Hopeful Plans

"For I know the plans that I have for you," declares the LORD, "plans for prosperity and not for disaster, to give you a future and a hope."

JEREMIAH 29:11 NASB

The plans of the Lord are lifegiving and hopeful for all who follow him. The compassionate one is able to take what others meant for evil and bring blessing through it. Suffering isn't meaningless. Pain isn't forever.

If you're having a hard time believing that God has good things for you, turn to him today. Remember his love, his kindness, and his grace. Remember where he's brought you, and look with eyes of grateful curiosity for the gifts you are experiencing that you once dreamt about.

Lord, when I am discouraged, remind me of how near, how intentional you are in kindness, and how capable you are to redeem what seems lost.

Scripture Reading: Jeremiah 33-36

Giver of Understanding

"Call to Me, and I will answer you, and show you great and mighty things, which you do not know."
JEREMIAH 33:3 NKJV

It's not a bad place to be when we realize we don't know something. The beginning of wisdom is admitting what we don't know and humbling ourselves before the one who does. He is eager to instruct us as we turn to him.

The Holy Spirit is our teacher. God doesn't expect us to retain all the information we've ever taken in. That's impossible! As long as we're listening and learning as we go, the Spirit will direct us and give us the wisdom we need for the moment.

Lord, I'm so glad I don't have to wait to call to you. I lift my voice, turn my gaze, and open my ears to listen.

Scripture Reading: Jeremiah 37-40

True Freedom

"Today I am freeing you from the chains on your wrists… Look, the whole country is open to you. Go wherever you wish."

Jeremiah 40:4 NCV

True freedom offers choice. In Christ, we find ourselves fully loved and set free. We then have the opportunity to choose where we will go, what we will do, and how we will live. It is for freedom that Christ set us free, so let's wisely choose what it is we do with that freedom.

God's gift of grace is free for all who will come to him and take it. He doesn't weigh us down with heavy expectations or look for us to pay him back. We couldn't if we tried! What we choose to do with our freedom is up to us. Why not use our freedom for goodness, peace, and joy?

Lord, thank you for the power of choice. It is a gift, and I don't take it lightly.

Scripture Reading: Jeremiah 41-44

Prayerful Direction

"Pray that the LORD your God will tell us where we should go and what we should do."

JEREMIAH 42:3 NIV

God willingly directs all who seek his guidance. Even if we're not accustomed to asking for God's help, today is a great time to start. We can also support others in prayer. God shares his wisdom with those who seek it.

When we feel at our weakest, those are the most necessary times to press into God's presence. God doesn't need our strength. He meets us in our frailty and shows us the way forward. He knows which paths to take, which people to talk to, and exactly what needs to be done in any situation.

Wise God, you are the one I look to, and I trust you will guide me with your wisdom.

Scripture Reading: Jeremiah 45-48

Promise of Peace

"I will bring you home again from distant lands,
and your children will return from their exile.
Israel will return to a life of peace and quiet,
and no one will terrorize them."

JEREMIAH 46:27 NLT

Though we cannot escape hard times, there is always hope in God's promises. He has not stopped moving in restorative mercy, and every promise he has made will be fulfilled. Going through a difficult season? There's hope on the other side and peace in his presence. You can rely on him to meet you in the mess and lead you out into fields of restoration where you can rest.

We don't have to wait for everything to calm down to experience God's peace. When we've prayed and thanked God, his peace transcends understanding.

Present One, be near. Settle my anxious thoughts in your peace.

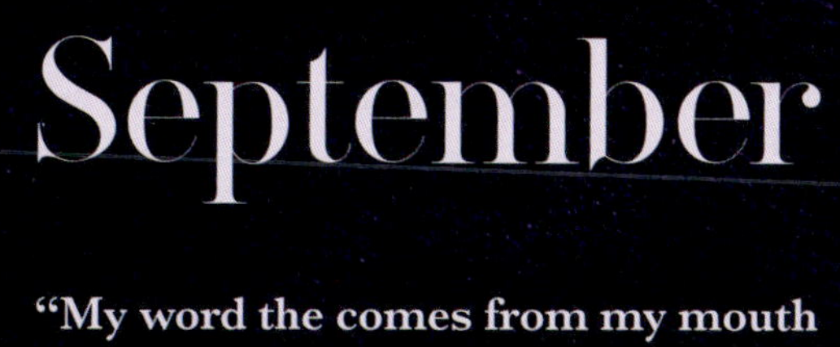

September

"My word the comes from my mouth
will not return to me empty,
but it will accomplish what I please
and will prosper in what I send it to do."

Isaiah 55:11 CSB

Scripture Reading: Jeremiah 49-52

Room for Restoration

"Afterward I will restore the fortunes of the Ammonites."
JEREMIAH 49:6 ESV

No one is without room for hope or restoration in Christ. Even what was taken away can be restored in the powerful presence of God's grace. God always makes room for mercy, no matter who you are or what you've done. And mercy makes all things new.

May you have eyes to see hope where you have only seen despair and ears to hear the song of redemption God sings over you. All may seem lost, but it is not. There is always grace, mercy, and peace ready to meet you as you come to the Lord with a humble heart.

Redeemer, breathe your Spirit of hope over my heart, mind, and life today. I need your perspective to clear up my own.

Scripture Reading: Lamentations 1-3

New Every Morning

Because of the LORD's faithful love
we do not perish,
for his mercies never end.
They are new every morning;
great is your faithfulness!
LAMENTATIONS 3:21-23 CSB

God's faithful love doesn't waver, and it doesn't diminish. His mercies are new every morning! Look to the sunrise as a reminder of fresh hope, present mercy, and generous grace. God is near, and he is waiting to pour his love over you.

When you are troubled, there is hope. When you are worried, God's faithfulness has not changed. Call this to mind whenever you need a perspective shift! The resurrection power of Christ is your eternal hope!

God, I bring you the worries and anxieties I can't shake. I trade them for your peace.

Scripture Reading: Lamentations 4-5

King Eternal

You, LORD, rule forever;
Your throne is from generation to generation.
LAMENTATIONS 5:19 NASB

Kingdoms rise and fall, but God is steadfast. Powerful regimes topple. There is no earthly government that withstands the breadth of time, but God's kingdom is eternal. He rules and reigns from generation to generation, and he will never fail.

Everything will be made right in the realm of God's perfect kingdom, but until we meet God face-to-face, we must trust that his power meets us in the challenges we face. No powers of earth can stand against him and prevail. He is the Creator of all and the King eternal.

Eternal One, you name is the name by which every knee will bow and every tongue confess. May that day come soon!

Scripture Reading: Ezekiel 1-4

Under His Hand

The hand of the LORD was upon me there, and He said to me, "Arise, go out into the plain, and there I shall talk with you."

EZEKIEL 3:22 NKJV

When we seek God, he reveals himself to us. When we listen for his voice, we will know when to stay and when to go. He directs our steps, and he reveals his plans. It is a privilege to be under the hand of God, hearing his voice and responding to his direction. Let's not take it for granted!

Today is the day to turn to the Lord and hear his voice. He has specific wisdom to share with you that will directly influence your steps. You won't be confused as you follow him, for the path is lit with his radiant glory.

Lord, I want to be under your guiding hand. Speak, for I am listening.

Scripture Reading: Ezekiel 5-8

You Will Know

"Then you will know that I am the LORD."

EZEKIEL 7:4 NCV

Whether in hard times or in good, God reveals himself to us. There are consequences to our actions, and we can't escape them. We can, however, know God more as we submit ourselves to his correction and seek to make things right.

God promises to make every wrong right, and we can count on him to do it. Let's pursue his ways all the days of our lives so that we stand in his righteous presence with confidence. He is worthy of our submission, and we can trust his love in every season.

God, I want to walk so closely with you that your path of love is all I know.

Scripture Reading: Ezekiel 9-12

A Tender Heart

"I will give them an undivided heart
and put a new spirit in them;
I will remove from them their heart of stone
and give them a heart of flesh."
EZEKIEL 11:19 NIV

A hardened heart is dangerous because we cannot choose what we become rigid about and what we remain open to. We need the power of God's love to melt our cold hearts. God calls us to be tender and compassionate because he is tender and compassionate.

Look to the life of Christ for the greatest living example of God's mercy in action. He humbled himself where others stoked their own egos in pride. He served the sick, and he befriended sinners. He wants us to walk in his ways, increases the tenderness of our hearts.

Lord, give me an undivided heart and put a new spirit in me.

Scripture Reading: Ezekiel 13-16

A Day for Turning

"Tell the people of Israel, 'This is what the Sovereign LORD says: Repent and turn away from your idols, and stop all your detestable sins.'"

EZEKIEL 14:6 NLT

Repentance is a big deal to God. He gives us every opportunity to turn from the things that bring us further from love and deeper into captivity. He is the Savior who sets us free and turns our darkest nights into bright mornings of relief and celebration. But he doesn't do this without our permission. We have to want the change. We have to choose to turn away from what's holding us back and come to the Father humbly. He understands us better than we know, so why remain at a distance for fear of what turning away means? We gain far greater treasure by turning toward him and yielding to his care.

Lord, I don't want to stay stuck in shackles of my own choosing. I want to walk in the light and liberty of your ways.

Scripture Reading: Ezekiel 17-20

Turn and Live

"I have no pleasure in the death of anyone, declares the LORD God; so turn, and live."

EZEKIEL 18:32 ESV

God does not delight in destruction. He doesn't want anyone to perish. He longs for all to come to him and live. God gave us free will, and that means that it is our choice how we will live. We can choose to live in corruption, fear, or hatred, or we can choose to turn to the Lord and receive his mercy that transforms us.

We have little to lose in this life and much to gain in God's kingdom when we turn to him. He is better than anything we have tasted, and his faithful mercy knows no end. Let's turn to him and live.

Lord God, I don't want to be stubborn. I know your way is the way of life. I choose to turn to you and live.

Scripture Reading: Ezekiel 21-24

Stand in the Gap

"I searched for a man among them who would repair the wall and stand in the gap before me on behalf of the land so that I might not destroy it, but I found no one."

EZEKIEL 22:30 CSB

What does it mean to stand in the gap on behalf of others? God is looking for people to intercede. We can volunteer our time, attention, and compassion to pray for those who need his mercy.

Intercession is a gift of connection, and it moves God's heart. We'd be hard-pressed to intercede in prayer for someone and remain unmoved by God's compassion for them. It is as much for us as it is for them that we make intercession a practice. When you see a need, use it as fuel for prayer today. When you see a gap, stand there and intercede.

Lord, I want to be a gap-filler in your kingdom. As I pray for others, move my heart and your hand on their behalf.

Scripture Reading: Ezekiel 25-28

Songs for Seasons

"You, son of man, take up a song of mourning."
EZEKIEL 27:2 NASB

Ecclesiastes reminds us there is a season for everything under heaven. There is a time for celebration and mourning. When there is reason to grieve, let's not pretend that everything is alright. God knows the truth of suffering, pain, and oppression, and he doesn't want us to ignore them.

There will be times when we are moved to take up a song of mourning. Let's not resist that when it comes. What is ignored cannot be healed. A wound left to fester will not get better by neglect. God is our healer. He meets us in our pain and ministers to us there. While we wait for his healing, let's not shrink back from expressing the true sorrow that is present.

Lord, I don't want to ignore the realities of suffering. Thank you for allowing me space to grieve while I wait for your healing.

Scripture Reading: Ezekiel 29-32

Humble Hearts

"Those who uphold Egypt shall fall,
And the pride of her power shall come down."
EZEKIEL 30:6 NKJV

It is dangerous territory to mix our faith with confidence in powers on the earth. Pride always goes before a fall: this is as true for nations and governments as it is for individuals. Let's humble our hearts before the Lord and follow the simple power of his gospel truth.

The systems of this earth will fail us every time. Let's be wary of people who use pride like a weapon, oppressing the vulnerable and manipulating systems for their own gain. This is not the way of God, nor is it the promise of God's kingdom. Let's uphold our humble Savior and the wisdom of God that stands the test of time.

Lord, I don't want to trust in systems of this world more than I trust in you. You are the one who humbles the proud and uplifts the humble. I choose your ways.

Scripture Reading: Ezekiel 33-36

Best Leader

"I will bless them and let them live around my hill. I will cause the rains to come when it is time; there will be showers to bless them."

EZEKIEL 34:26 NCV

God takes care of the vulnerable and oppressed. Few leaders in positions of power do this. Many care more for their pride, power, and bottom line than they do taking care of others. This isn't the way of God's kingdom, nor is it the way he chooses to lead.

He has given us Jesus Christ as our eternal shepherd who cares for us. He tends to us, and we can trust his heart and his intentions. He will never misuse his power, abuse us, or misdirect us. He is full of loving truth, hopeful peace, and faithful goodness. We can trust his leadership.

Trusted Leader, the greatest blessings are found in you and in your care. Shower me with the blessings of your presence today.

Scripture Reading: Ezekiel 37-40

Home

"I will put my Spirit in you and you will live, and I will settle you in your own land."

Ezekiel 37:14 NIV

The life-giving Spirit of God is available to all who come to the Father through Christ. The Holy Spirit is our burden-lifter, teacher, and wise counselor. He is our comforter, peace-giver, and perspective-shifter. There is so much love in his presence!

No matter where we go, God's Spirit has already made his home in us. He also sets us in places in this world with connections that are like family, where we can care for each other. We are home in him wherever we are, but we also find ourselves at home in specific places in this world.

Lord, you are my home, and I am a home for your presence. You are here with me.

Scripture Reading: Ezekiel 41-44

Glimpses of Glory

I looked and saw that the glory of the LORD filled the Temple of the LORD, and I fell face down on the ground.

EZEKIEL 44:4 NLT

There are moments in our walk with God that he pulls back the curtain between this realm and his kingdom, and we catch glimpses of his glory. These encounters with his greatness mark us. They leave us in awe, for the light that radiates from his presence is astounding.

When we are in the presence of something greater than ourselves, we can feel the stirring of awe in. These are beautiful gifts that we can remember throughout our lifetime. God reveals himself to those who seek him, so let's make knowing him our aim. As we do, we will see his glory, and it will change us.

Glorious One, I seek you, for you are worthy of my praise every moment of every day.

Scripture Reading: Ezekiel 45-48

Rivers of Living Water

"Everything will live where the river goes."
EZEKIEL 47:9 ESV

God is our true source. He is our peace, strength, joy, and hope. Every practical need is met in abundance. Every desire is fulfilled in the power of his love. God himself is our light, our salvation, and the source of every good and perfect gift. He is the essence of life itself.

Have we come to the rivers of living water and danced in its depths? Jesus is our source of living water that satisfies our souls. He is all we need and more than we realize we want in this life. He is better than we've yet known, and he is pursuing us. Let's wade into the river of life.

Source of Life, thank you that everything I need is found in you. I enter your river of life and let the flow of your waters carry me.

Scripture Reading: Daniel 1-4

In the Fire

"Look! I see four men, not tied, walking around in the fire unharmed; and the fourth looks like a son of the gods."

DANIEL 3:25 CSB

There were four in the furnace, but only three went in. God was in the fire with Meshach, Shadrach, and Abednego. This wasn't some small fire; it was an incinerator. The servants that carried the three men up died because the flames overtook them. It was nothing less than a supernatural miracle that saved these lovers of God.

When you find yourself in impossible situations, God is with you too. Trust him to deliver you. When you ask for his help, he will not abandon you. He goes with you into the hardest trials you face. As you continue to choose his ways, he will honor you. You can count on his faithful presence.

Lord, in fires of testing, be near. Protect me and deliver me from situations that are meant to harm me, but I did nothing to deserve. I trust you.

Scripture Reading: Daniel 5-8

Vindicated

"My God sent His angel and shut the lions' mouths, and they have not harmed me, since I was found innocent before Him; and also toward you, O king, I have committed no crime."

DANIEL 6:22 NASB

Though the king liked Daniel, he could not ignore the accusations made against him. Daniel spent a night in the lion's den, where he should have been devoured, but God intervened. He shut the mouths of the lions, and Daniel was lifted from the den in the morning, not only safe but vindicated.

When others make false accusations against us, we don't have to defend ourselves. We can tell the truth, and trust that it will come out. The Lord always knows the truth. He never misunderstands us, and he can't be turned against us with manipulative tactics. He doesn't believe liars because he sees right through them.

Lord, it is painful to be falsely accused, yet you always know the truth. Reveal it in your perfect time.

Scripture Reading: Daniel 9-12

Great Mercies

We do not present our supplications before You because of our righteous deeds, but because of Your great mercies.
DANIEL 9:18 NKJV

We appeal to God based on his nature not our own. That means no matter where we are in the world, no matter what we face, we can trust that he hears us because he is merciful. When we come before him with hearts that are true and seeking, he cannot help but turn toward us.

God is full of mercy, and it is that mercy we stand upon in our prayers. We don't have to beg him to hear us. We only have to appeal to his nature, for we already know who he is: patient, merciful, and gracious. Let's bring our prayers and stand upon the foundation of his never-failing love.

Merciful God, I am so glad that you are unchanging. It is because of who you are that I know you, and it is because of your mercy that I'm here.

Scripture Reading: Hosea 1-4

Children of God

"They were called, 'You are not my people,'
but later they will be called 'children of the living God.'"
HOSEA 1:10 NCV

It doesn't matter who we are or where we come from, when we take God's invitation to know him, we become one of his own. He adopts us as his children, and everything about us is under the covering of his powerful mercy.

Shame can keep us stuck in old identities, but God wants us to live in the freedom of his passionate love. He is full of kindness and grace, and we never need to fear his reaction when we come to him. Whatever we have been called in this life, God gives us a new name when we enter his family. What can come against us when our identity is found in him?

God, you are my perfect Father. I am grateful to be yours.

Scripture Reading: Hosea 5-8

As Surely as the Dawn

"Let us acknowledge the Lord;
let us press on to acknowledge him.
As surely as the sun rises,
he will appear;
he will come to us like the winter rains,
like the spring rains that water the earth."
Hosea 6:3 NIV

God's faithfulness is sure. We can count on his redemption power to meet us as we acknowledge the truth of who he is. It is good to build the practice of daily turning our hearts toward him. He is even more reliable than the sun.

Let's look to the cues of nature to remind us of the power of God. There is so much to learn about him in the everyday things we overlook.

Lord, you are more constant than the air I breathe, more reliable than the rising sun, and closer than the skin on my bones. Open my eyes to the wonders of who you are through this natural world.

Scripture Reading: Hosea 9-11

Good Seeds

"Plant the good seeds of righteousness,
and you will harvest a crop of love.
Plow up the hard ground of your hearts,
for now is the time to seek the LORD,
that he may come
and shower righteousness upon you."
HOSEA 10:12 NLT

Good fruit does not appear by accident. It is cultivated. Seeds of surrender lead to the fruit of the same. It might feel bitter to plant it, but the fruit is sweet. Seeds of righteousness lead to a crop of love.

As we tend to the ground of our hearts, turning over the soil to soften it, the Lord meets us in the work. His compassion loosens the dirt, and his peace enriches the soil. Where seeds of his truth are planted will come a harvest of his wisdom.

Lord, you are the heavenly gardener, and you know everything I need to thrive in this life.

Scripture Reading: Hosea 12-14

Active Waiting

"You, by the help of your God, return,
hold fast to love and justice,
and wait continually for your God."
HOSEA 12:6 ESV

Waiting isn't a one-and-done experience. While we sojourn through this life, we continue to wait on the Lord. We are living in the in-between space of faith and fulfillment. This requires our active patience, pursuit, and trust.

How we wait reveals a great deal about what we believe. If we believe that God is faithful, we will lean into that. If we believe that he is kind, we won't hesitate to turn to him, no matter how much we've failed. If we believe that he is patient, we don't have to rush things along on our own. As we wait, let's press into his presence.

Near One, I want to learn to wait well. That hasn't always been true, but I trust you are actively transforming me by your love as I wait on you.

Scripture Reading: Joel 1-3

Spirit Gifts

"I will pour out my Spirit on all humanity;
then your sons and your daughters will prophesy,
your old men will have dreams,
and your young men will see visions."
JOEL 2:28 CSB

The promise of the Spirit's outpouring is upon us. We didn't miss it. Jesus' followers experienced this outpouring, as recorded in the Book of Acts. The Holy Spirit is as accessible to us today as he was then.

First Corinthians 12 talks about various spiritual gifts offered to God's people. These are things we don't have to strive for; they come directly from God. He pours his Spirit on us, and there is supernatural discernment and wisdom given through prophesies, dreams, and visions. It doesn't matter how young, old, or experienced we are; the gifts of the Spirit come to all who wait.

Holy Spirit, pour over me as I wait on you.

Scripture Reading: Amos 1-3

God Reveals Himself

Certainly the LORD God does nothing
Unless He reveals His secret plan
To His servants the prophets.
AMOS 3:7 NASB

God doesn't act without revealing his intentions. He doesn't move without warning. His plans are actively coming together, and he gives us opportunities to respond. He gives chance upon chance to repent, to turn to him and away from sin. Those who are found in him will find refuge.

God's ways are not hidden. It requires effort to know him, to listen to him, and to walk out his ways. But the way of the Lord is life-giving. He restores, refreshes, and strengthens us as we go.

Lord God, open my eyes to see who you are and what you are doing.

Scripture Reading: Amos 4-6

Live

"Seek Me and live;
Seek good and not evil,
That you may live."
AMOS 5:4,14 NKJV

True life is found in God. As we seek good and turn away from evil, life is our promised reward. There is nothing to escape or hide in the light of God's love. When we walk in the light of integrity, we also have nothing to hide.

Justice, honesty, and goodness are key indicators that we walk in the way of Christ. We don't have to speak perfectly or know exactly what is needed in any moment, but to seek the Lord and choose to align ourselves with the fruit of God's Spirit. As we love, extend grace, have compassion, and pursue peace, we reflect the light of God alive within us.

Lord, I want to come alive in your energizing light of love and reflect your goodness through my actions.

Scripture Reading: Amos 7-9

Rebuilder

"The kingdom of David is like a fallen tent,
but in that day I will set it up again
and mend its broken places.
I will rebuild its ruins
as it was before."

AMOS 9:11 NCV

God is the rebuilder of ruins. When we are in the middle of a shaking, where everything seems to be falling apart, it can feel defeating. In our disheartened disappointment, we might be tempted to feel like we've reached the end.

When we can see no way out or through, God shines the light of his hope on us. He will rebuild what's broken down. He will restore what earthly talent cannot touch. He will do what no one else can. He does it in the mercy of his timing. Let's look to our eternal hope today for a glimpse of his goodness, for surely he never fails.

Restorer, breathe your hope into my heart and mind today, and lift the weight of my disappointment.

Scripture Reading: Obadiah 1

A Right Heart

"You should not gloat over your brother
in the day of his misfortune,
nor rejoice over the people of Judah
in the day of their destruction,
nor boast so much
in the day of their trouble."

OBADIAH 1:12 NIV

It's not godly to rejoice in someone else's misfortune. When we celebrate the destruction of others, we reveal our hearts. God wants restoration. He is just, yes, but that does not mean he is unmoved by compassion.

There is relief when justice is served. It's not that we shouldn't feel or celebrate that. But God is still merciful; he is still kind. May we choose his kindness even over those we have seen as enemies. Let's keep our hearts covered in compassion while praying for justice.

Lord, teach me to be more like you. May I remain humble, compassionate, and kind in every situation.

Scripture Reading: Jonah 1-4

He Answers

"I cried out to the LORD in my great trouble,
and he answered me.
I called to you from the land of the dead,
and LORD, you heard me!"
JONAH 2:2 NLT

Even when Jonah was running away from God's direction, he was not too far from God's presence. Jonah cried out, and the Lord answered. He still answers our cries today. Even when we run from him, he does not abandon us.

Jonah knew God's character as he complained that God would turn with compassion toward those Jonah didn't think were worth sparing. Let's join God's heart and rejoice when he answers the cries of those who turn to him.

Lord, you are the God who answers with mercy. May I embrace your compassion, not only for myself but for all who turn to you.

Scripture Reading: Micah 1-4

Straighten Up

"Has the LORD grown impatient?
Are these his deeds?
Do not my words do good
to him who walks uprightly?"
MICAH 2:7 ESV

Those who walk in the ways of God, who uphold justice, mercy, and grace are those who walk uprightly. When we walk in the way of integrity, allowing the heart of God to move us in compassion toward others, we have nothing to fear.

When others are being called to account for their hypocrisy, let us be found as those who didn't let the cloak of God's love slip from our shoulders. Pride leads to downfall. Selfishness leads to isolation, fear, and self-protection. Humble hearts lead to the Father, and they are led by his gracious hand.

Lord, open my eyes to where I have let other influences lead me away from love. I choose to return to your path of righteousness.

Scripture Reading: Micah 5-7

What Is Good

"Mankind, he has told each of you what is good
and what it is the LORD requires of you:
to act justly,
to love faithfulness,
and to walk humbly with your God."
MICAH 6:8 CSB

The requirements of the Lord are not easy, but they are also not too much to bear. He's not looking for perfection. What we cannot do on our own, we can do through the strength of God's Spirit alive in us. If we will submit ourselves to following him, he will help us along the way.

When we walk humbly with God, he is able to teach us and redirect us. He doesn't punish us for mistakes, but calls us up and shows us how to do better. When we act impartially, uphold faithfulness, and maintain humility, we reflect the love of God.

Lord, help me to walk in your ways and to do good every day.

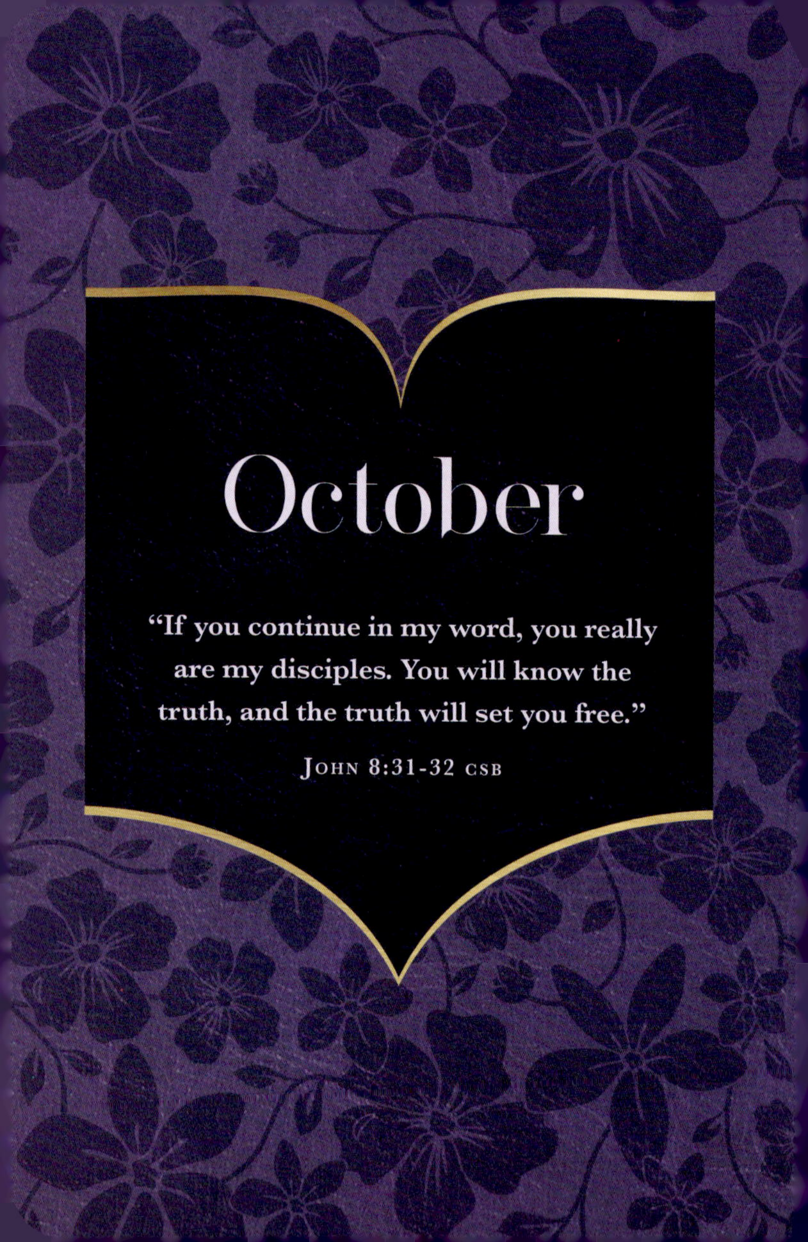
October
"If you continue in my word, you really are my disciples. You will know the truth, and the truth will set you free."
John 8:31-32 CSB

Scripture Reading: Nahum 1-3

The Goodness of God

The LORD is good,
A stronghold in the day of trouble,
And He knows those who take refuge in Him.

NAHUM 1:7 NASB

God will not let those who plan against him stand. His Word prevails, and his justice will roll like a mighty river. Yet, he remains a stronghold for those who take refuge in him. He is a safe place for all who run into his heart to find respite.

The Lord is good, and his goodness is revealed in his truth. He redeems those who escape cycles of sin by turning to him. He is better than we know, and we can know him more each day. Let's not forget to hide ourselves in him when we can't escape the troubles of this world.

Lord, you are good. Hide me in the shelter of your presence, and settle my worries in your peace.

Scripture Reading: Habakkuk 1-3

Look and See

"Look among the nations and watch—
Be utterly astounded!
For I will work a work in your days
Which you would not believe, though it were told you."
HABAKKUK 1:5 NKJV

God's miraculous ways astound us. If we look for what he is doing in the world, we will witness his love that awakens our hearts in awe. He is always moving in the details. He is not absent when we cannot see his movement on the surface. When his love breaks through, it is undeniable.

God loves to meet us in ways that fill us with wonder. He is more kind, detailed, and intentional than anyone who has ever lived. Let's raise our level of expectation as we wait in anticipation of what he will do next. He is on the move, and he is doing a work that will leave us breathless!

Miraculous One, thank you for not giving up when most would. I wait in holy expectation of your love.

Scripture Reading: Zephaniah 1-3

The Joy of the Lord

"The Lord your God is with you;
the mighty One will save you.
He will rejoice over you.
You will rest in his love;
he will sing and be joyful about you."
Zephaniah 3:17 NCV

God delights in restoring his people. He loves to save those who cry out to him. He always meets the humble of heart and helps those who call out to him. He sees you, he knows you, and he loves you. You don't have to doubt it.

The Lord rejoices over his children. He delights in us. All who come to him to find rest will be satisfied, and what's more, they will know the power of his affection.

Lord my God, you are my help, my strength, and my resting place. Open my ears that I might hear the melody of your delight.

Scripture Reading: Haggai 1-2

Even Better

"'The glory of this present house will be greater than the glory of the former house,' says the LORD Almighty. 'And in this place I will grant peace,' declares the LORD Almighty."

HAGGAI 2:9 NIV

God doesn't restore things to what they were before; his redemption makes things better. No matter what we face, we can take hope in the eternal goodness of God. What is coming is better than we've known. This will always remain true, for the fullness of God's presence is with us in the present, and it goes before us until we rest in the glorious reality of his kingdom.

We go from glory to glory in Christ Jesus. We have not left our best days behind. Though life brings many changes, God remains increasingly good and forever faithful. He continues to create powerful fruit in our surrendered lives.

Almighty God, there is no one else like you. Encourage my heart in hope as I set my eyes upon you.

Scripture Reading: Zechariah 1-4

Return

"Return to me, and I will return to you, says the LORD of Heaven's Armies."

ZECHARIAH 1:3 NLT

Though God waits for us to move toward him, that doesn't mean he's not already closely watching us. He's waiting with hopeful expectation, just as we do when we turn toward him. As soon as we make our way toward him, he runs to meet us.

God is ready to meet you, and he only needs your willingness. Even the slightest turn toward him, and you will be able to see that he is waiting. He is watching. He is ready to restore, support, and cover you with the robes of his righteousness. Return today; don't wait a moment longer!

Righteous One, I don't want to dig in my heels in resistance. I am open, I am curious, and I am wanting your life-giving love. I turn toward you today. Thank you for meeting me as I do.

Scripture Reading: Zechariah 5-8

Blessings and Strength

"As you have been a byword of cursing… so will I save you, and you shall be a blessing. Fear not, but let your hands be strong."

ZECHARIAH 8:13 ESV

No matter what others think of you, God's mercy can change everything. Don't abandon his ways or walk away from his love. He will restore you. He will save you, and he will make you a blessing to those who once cursed you.

Don't fear what others say. That's a reflection of them and not of you. Walk in the light of God's love and depend on his defense, and you will have no reason to fear. Turn your hesitance to courage, and strengthen your hands as you continue to do the work the Lord has called you to do.

Savior, I won't give up walking the path of your love. This is where I come alive. I trust you to defend me.

Scripture Reading: Zechariah 9-11

Ask for It

Ask the LORD for rain
in the season of spring rain.
The LORD makes the rain clouds,
and he will give them showers of rain
and crops in the field for everyone.
ZECHARIAH 10:1 CSB

Ask the Lord for what you need, for he gives rain and sun in their turn. He is the one who set the earth into motion, and he delights in answering the prayers of his people. Don't hold back your prayers, thinking God is too busy to hear. He listens for your voice, and he answers every time.

Will you trust God to meet you? Will you ask him to provide the things that you need to succeed? His resources are abundant, and you can't reach the end of them. He loves to give good gifts to his children, so don't hold back today.

Lord, I don't want to withhold asking you for what I need in this life. You are my provider, and I trust you.

Scripture Reading: Zechariah 12-14

Christ Our King

The LORD will be King over all the earth; on that day the LORD will be the only one, and His name the only one.

ZECHARIAH 14:9 NASB

The prophetic picture of Christ is all over the book of Zechariah. In this verse, we are reminded that there will be only one King over all. He is the Lord of lords, and the King of kings. He will reign in justice, mercy, and eternal peace.

Jesus Christ is our Lord, and he will be King over all the earth. Until we wait for the fulfillment of his coming, we can take hope and live under his reign by humbling our hearts and following his ways. We can pledge our allegiance to him before every knee bows and confesses that he is Lord. We get to choose this day whom we'll serve. So, let's serve the King of glory!

Jesus Christ, you are King over all, and you reign in righteousness. I bow my knee before you in humble surrender.

Scripture Reading: Malachi 1-4

Unchanging One

"I am the LORD, I do not change;
Therefore you are not consumed, O sons of Jacob."
MALACHI 3:6 NKJV

It is God's unchanging nature that we stand upon as our confidence. We can put our faith in him, for he is trustworthy and true. His mercy reaches us no matter where we are or what we've done. His grace is available in this moment, just as every other moment. He is our present help, and he remains faithful.

Let's continue to honor the Lord in our lives, surrendering our hearts in wholehearted trust. He will do as he promised, and he will shine on us with the light of his healing love.

Unfailing One, you don't change, and that is exceedingly good news. Strengthen my heart in hope as you meet me with your persistent mercy.

Scripture Reading: Matthew 1-4

Light of the World

"These people who live in darkness
will see a great light."
MATTHEW 4:16 NCV

Jesus is the great light prophesied about in Isaiah. He is the Living Word. The New Testament is a new beginning. It is a new chapter in the dawning of God's wisdom. Here we find the beautiful life of Jesus and encouragement to follow him. He is the revelation of the Father, and in his life we see the light.

Have you experienced Jesus as a light that shines in the darkness? Has he turned the shadows of shame, fear, and confusion to peace, order, and gratitude in his presence? May you know the light of the world and follow him.

Lord Jesus, I long to know you more and to walk in the light of your life.

Scripture Reading: Matthew 5-8

Seek First

"Seek first his kingdom and his righteousness, and all these things will be given to you as well."
MATTHEW 6:33 NIV

We don't have to worry about what we'll eat, drink, or wear when we follow God. He promises to take care of our needs. When we concern ourselves with seeking his kingdom, and walking in his ways, we are assured that everything else we need will be provided too.

God doesn't want us to ignore the desires of our hearts, but he also doesn't want us to be consumed by them. Take delight in God, and everything else becomes like frosting on a cake. He will provide for your needs, and he will satisfy your desires.

Lord Jesus, I seek you first today. May everything I need, and more than I know to ask for, meet me as I follow you. I trust you.

Scripture Reading: Matthew 9-12

Find Rest

"Come to me, all of you who are weary and carry heavy burdens, and I will give you rest. Take my yoke upon you. Let me teach you, because I am humble and gentle at heart, and you will find rest for your souls."

MATTHEW 11:28-29 NLT

Jesus offers to lighten our loads and carry our burdens. Why would we refuse him? As we bring him our heavy burdens of worry, he lifts them. He tells us to take his yoke upon our shoulders. This is what partnership looks like. He offers us one side of the yoke to help carry, but the wonderfully gracious part is he does all the heavy lifting!

Jesus is a wise teacher, humble at heart, and always ready to speak the truth with love. In his gracious presence, we find rest for our souls. He leads us beside still waters to restore our souls.

Lord, I come to you for rest today. I don't want to carry the weight of troubles and worries. I offer them to you.

Scripture Reading: Matthew 13-16

Steady Encouragement

Jesus immediately reached out his hand and took hold of him, saying to him, "O you of little faith, why did you doubt?"

MATTHEW 14:31 ESV

Perhaps you don't read Jesus' response to Peter's wavering as encouragement. It was a teachable moment. Peter was the only one brave enough to step out of the boat to walk to Jesus. When fear overtook his heart, he began to sink, but Jesus was right there reaching out his hand to steady him. There was no real danger of him drowning.

Jesus, while taking hold of Peter, said, "O you of little faith, why did you doubt?" While it might seem like a rebuke, what if it were more like an honest question to open the possibilities of faith to his disciples?

Lord, I don't want to resist your challenges. I want to grow in faith, to grow strong in trust. You are faithful, regardless, and that is a beautiful truth.

Scripture Reading: Matthew 17-20

A Forgiving Heart

"Lord, how many times must I forgive my brother or sister who sins against me? As many as seven times?" "I tell you, not as many as seven," Jesus replied, "but seventy times seven."

Matthew 18:21-22 csb

Jesus' forgiveness doesn't have a limit. Whenever we come to him with a humble heart, he restores us. He asks that we do the same, and he does it for our good. God never requires anything of us that he did not first do. He leads by example.

When we look for the limits of our love, we put a boundary on what God can do. He wants us to expand in his love. He fills us with his perfect love, and we follow his direction. It might sound impossible to forgive someone seventy times seven. The point wasn't that there be an exact number; it was that we shouldn't keep count! We should be quick to forgive to keep our hearts free from bitterness and full of love.

Lord, thank you for your endless love that keeps expanding my capacity.

Scripture Reading: Matthew 21-24

Greatness in Humility

"The greatest of you shall be your servant. Whoever exalts himself shall be humbled, and whoever humbles himself shall be exalted."

MATTHEW 23:11-12 NASB

The kingdom of Christ isn't about how much power or influence you have. Jesus flipped the script. He said the greatest would be the servants, and whoever humbles himself will be exalted. We see this in the life of Joseph in the Old Testament, and of other faithful followers of God. His ways haven't changed, and his priorities haven't either. He still looks at the heart.

Humility isn't pretending to be something we're not. It's not low self-esteem. Humility is a willingness to learn, to change our ways, and to walk in the way of love.

Humble King, you are the servant of all, leading in love. I choose to follow your ways and humble myself before you and others.

Scripture Reading: Matthew 25-28

He Is Risen

"He is not here; for He is risen, as He said. Come, see the place where the Lord lay."

MATTHEW 28:6 NKJV

Jesus did not stay in the tomb after they laid him there. On the third day, he rose in resurrection life. It is that very power that sets us free and brings us close to the Father. Jesus did just as he promised. Even when he shared with his disciples that he would die, they did not seem to believe him. They felt all was lost.

But Jesus did not stay in the grave. He may have suffered greatly, but he conquered death and removed the curse that it had over us. We now live in the power of his resurrection! Death has no hold over us, and fear has lost its grip.

Lord Jesus, I hold onto hope with a firm grasp. You are alive, and you are coming soon.

Scripture Reading: Mark 1-4

Peace Be Still

Jesus stood up and commanded the wind and said to the waves, "Quiet! Be still!" Then the wind stopped, and it became completely calm.

MARK 4:39 NCV

The disciples feared for their lives during this storm. It wasn't a little rain and some rocking of the boat. Jesus slept soundly through it because he had the confidence of the Father. He knew his time had not come yet, and he was able to rest. When the storms are raging, we can know the peace that passes understanding. Even more, we can call out and Jesus can calm the storm on our behalf.

Jesus had the authority to calm the wind and waves, and he still holds that power today. He speaks to the raging storm, and everything settles at his authoritative word. Did you know God can settle the storms in your mind, heart, and life too?

Jesus, speak peace over my heart, mind, and body today.

Scripture Reading: Mark 5-8

Faith that Heals

He said to her, "Daughter, your faith has healed you. Go in peace and be freed from your suffering."

MARK 5:34 NIV

The woman who approached Jesus and touched the hem of his garment had faith that led her to him. She didn't want to bother him, and she believed that if she could just touch a piece of his clothing, that the power to heal would come over her. Can you imagine such desperate determination?

It was no small thing, and it didn't go unnoticed. Jesus felt the power leave him, so he knew someone had touched him. When Jesus spoke to the woman, he assured her that it was her faith that healed her. Not only that, but he spoke a blessing of peace and freedom from her suffering.

Lord, may I have the tenacity of the woman who suffered in going after you. You are kind, you are generous, and you bless those who seek you.

Scripture Reading: Mark 9-12

Nothing Greater

"'Love the Lord your God with all your heart, all your soul, all your mind, and all your strength.' The second is equally important: 'Love your neighbor as yourself.' No other commandment is greater than these."

MARK 12:30-31 NLT

There is nothing greater, no act as powerful, as the act of loving God wholeheartedly and extending that love to others. Everything, the whole of the law of Moses, is encapsulated in the law of love. Whatever we do, let's put nothing above this mandate, for it is the foundation of the gospel. It is the essence of God himself.

If we will put our whole heart, soul, mind, and strength into loving God, everything else will work itself out.

Lord, you call us to love because that is what you do best and most faithfully. Thank you.

Scripture Reading: Mark 13-16

Thy Will Be Done

"Abba, Father, all things are possible for you. Remove this cup from me. Yet not what I will, but what you will."

MARK 14:36 ESV

Jesus knew what weakness was, and he felt the pang of not wanting to suffer. He went so far as to ask God to remove the cup of his suffering from him. Have you ever resisted what God was leading you through? You're not alone. It's okay to feel resistance and to bring it to the Lord in honest prayer.

When we pour our hearts out before the Lord, we don't have to censor ourselves. He knows the state of our hearts before we say a word. When we are troubled, let's take those troubles straight to the Lord in prayer. As we empty ourselves before him, may we end the same way Jesus did—in surrender.

Jesus, you submitted yourself to the Father's will, and I can submit myself to yours. I surrender.

Scripture Reading: Luke 1-4

Nothing Is Impossible

"Nothing will be impossible with God."
LUKE 1:37 CSB

God's abilities are beyond comprehension. He can bring babies out of barren wombs and life out of desolate places. He is able to do far more than we could ever think or imagine! Let's not limit his power according to what we've experienced. He can bring breakthrough in ways that astound us.

Bring God your impossible situations. Set them down before him, and invite him to meet you in those places. Trust him to do what only he can do, and believe that he will make a way where there seems to be none. Nothing is impossible with God.

Miraculous One, there is nothing you cannot do! May my faith grow to meet your faithfulness.

Scripture Reading: Luke 5-8

Willing

"Lord, if You are willing, You can make me clean." And He reached out with His hand and touched him, saying, "I am willing; be cleansed."

LUKE 5:12-13 NASB

Not only is God able to heal, but he is willing! There is a distinction here. Just because you can do something, it doesn't mean you're always eager to do it. Jesus is a kind and ready healer. He is able to do far more than we can imagine, but it's important to also recognize he is willing.

If we knew God were willing to meet us with powerful compassion, would we hold back from him? We know that God is merciful. It's in his nature. But are we convinced that love motivates him? Are we sure of his willingness to heal, to save, and to set free? May we be encouraged to come to him in faith, asking him to move.

Savior, help me to never withhold my own prayers for fear of how I'll be received. You are both able and willing to move in me.

Scripture Reading: Luke 9-12

Good Giver

"If you then, being evil, know how to give good gifts to your children, how much more will your heavenly Father give the Holy Spirit to those who ask Him!"

LUKE 11:13 NKJV

God gives good gifts to his children. He doesn't just meet the bare minimum of our needs, nor does he demand we thank him at every turn. He takes care of us as a loving parent. He is even more dependable, more generous, and more consistent than any earthly parent could be.

When you ask for the Holy Spirit, you can be sure that you will receive him. Ask, and you shall receive. Seek, and you will find. Knock, and the door will be opened to you. The Holy Spirit will meet you with the power of God's presence, transforming you from the inside out.

Lord, you give exceedingly good gifts. I ask for your Holy Spirit to be at home in me.

Scripture Reading: Luke 13-16

There Is Room

"People will come from the east, west, north, and south and will sit down at the table in the kingdom of God."
LUKE 13:29 NCV

There is room at the table of God's kingdom for all who come to him. Scripture says that people will come from all over. There will be believers from every nation, tribe, and language. God's kingdom is not a club we enter by earning our way. It is a family for all who need it. There is room for all who come to Christ in humble surrender.

No one can take your place at God's table, but you also must choose to come. God's invitation is available to you today. Will you enter the narrow gate through Christ and make yourself at home in his kingdom? There is room for you.

Savior, I won't wait along the fringes deciding what to do any longer. I come to you.

Scripture Reading: Luke 17-20

Never Give Up

Jesus told his disciples a parable to show them that they should always pray and not give up.

LUKE 18:1 NIV

How often do we give up at the first sign of resistance? Persistence is a powerful trait to have, especially when it comes to prayer. When there is something that's not easily granted, it doesn't mean it's time to give up. The only reason to give up is if it's not worth it.

The things that are worth it in life require persistence. Let's not let the passions of our heart grow cold. Let's not throw in the towel before we've received what we hope for. Some prayers will be answered quickly, and others will require persistence. Let's not give up going to the Lord and trusting his timing. He will move on our behalf as we keep pressing into his presence.

Lord, I don't want to give up easily on the things that truly matter. Help me to grow strong in perseverance and to keep pressing in for breakthrough.

Scripture Reading: Luke 21-24

Father Forgive Them

Jesus said, "Father, forgive them, for they don't know what they are doing."

LUKE 23:34 NLT

Even while the soldiers who crucified him were gambling to win his clothes, Jesus had compassion on them. He prayed for forgiveness because of their ignorance. How often do we pray for our enemies, for the people actively inflicting harm on us? How often do we forgive them and ask that they be forgiven?

This is a radical act of love. Let's ask the Lord to soften our hearts as we follow him. As his love transforms us, let us join with Jesus in asking forgiveness for those who know not what they do. We can pray that the Lord would open their eyes as we release forgiveness.

Merciful Father, I have so far to go in becoming more like Christ. Strengthen me to extend compassion in the face of violence and harm.

Scripture Reading: John 1-4

Grace upon Grace

From his fullness we have all received, grace upon grace.
John 1:16 esv

God offers us grace upon grace. That is good news. It means today, this moment, is an opportunity to receive more grace. We might question whether we've exhausted God's kindness. The truth is that God receives us with mercy and pours out his grace every time we come to him. That is all we must do: come to the Lord Jesus Christ with an open heart.

Take it one step at a time. What do you need today? What challenges are you facing? Can you bring it before the Lord and ask him to meet you in it? There is nothing he can't solve, and there is no problem he can't help you with.

Gracious One, thank you for receiving me with kindness, compassion, wisdom, and power every time I turn to you.

Scripture Reading: John 5-8

Truly Free

Jesus said to the Jews who had believed him, "If you continue in my word, you really are my disciples. You will know the truth, and the truth will set you free. So if the Son sets you free, you really will be free."

John 8:31-32,35 csb

The truth of Christ sets us free. It sets us free from condemnation, fear, and the myth of perfection. Jesus liberates all those who come to him in his powerful love, and we don't have to question our worth.

No matter the cycles we have struggled to break out of, the limits we have come up against, or the challenges of life that knocked us off our feet, Jesus remains the way, the truth, and the life. He doesn't free us to then saddle us down with fear or seek to manipulate us. We are free to live, and move, and have our being. He lifts our burdens and shows us the way to walk in the peace of his presence. He is so good!

Savior, you lift the weight of things I was never meant to carry alone, and you lead me into life.

Scripture Reading: John 9-12

Fullness of Life

"The thief comes only to steal and kill and destroy; I came so that they would have life, and have it abundantly."
JOHN 10:10 NASB

Jesus doesn't save us so we'll barely survive. He gives abundant life. In him, we are freed from fear, shame, and sin. We aren't just given a little grace to get us into his kingdom. We are given grace upon grace to sustain and strengthen us each day. He is present, he is faithful, and he is so very good!

In this world, there are forces that seek to steal, kill, and destroy. God is not one of those forces. He offers life in abundance. More than enough for each of us, no matter the season or the struggle.

Lord, you are my hope, my support, and my greatest joy. You are the source of every good thing, and I can't stay away.

Scripture Reading: John 13-15

Abide

"I am the vine, you are the branches. He who abides in Me, and I in him, bears much fruit; for without Me you can do nothing."

JOHN 15:5 NKJV

Abiding in Christ is an invitation to rest in him, to plant our roots in him, and to yield to his love. When we walk in his ways, we abide. When we receive his peace, we abide. When we offer grace to others, we abide.

A good fruit-filled life is evidence not of our own strength or goodness, but of the power of Christ's life empowering us. We don't have to try harder, to strive in our own strength, to produce the fruit of God's kingdom. When we plant ourselves in him, his love motivates everything we do.

Lord, you are the vine, and I am a branch abiding in you. You are my life-source and strength.

Scripture Reading: John 16-18

Grief to Joy

"I tell you the truth, it is better for you that I go away. When I go away, I will send the Helper to you. If I do not go away, the Helper will not come."

JOHN 16:7 NCV

Without what Jesus did, we would not have the constant presence of the Holy Spirit both with us and in us. When Jesus died on the cross, the veil that was in the temple separating the presence of God from the people was torn. It signified the separation between God and humans was over. In Christ, we are able to know God, and to have the power of the Spirit's presence in us.

What was cause for grief turned to joy. While we cannot skip the process of mourning our losses, we can be sure that there is beauty on the horizon. Where there is grief, it will be turned to joy. We can count on it!

Jesus, thank you for your sacrifice that made it possible to have the Holy Spirit as helper, teacher, and comforter.

November

The LORD gives wisdom;
from his mouth come knowledge
and understanding.

PROVERBS 2:6 CSB

Scripture Reading: John 19-21

Witness and Messenger

"Go instead to my brothers and tell them, 'I am ascending to my Father and your Father, to my God and your God.'"

JOHN 20:17 NIV

God met with women, honored them, and made them messengers of his goodness. Serving God has nothing to do with where you come from; it has everything to do with your pursuit of him. He reveals himself to those who seek him.

Mary Magdalene was at the tomb, weeping over the fact that she couldn't find Jesus' body. She was the first person Jesus revealed himself to, and it happened because she was there seeking him first. God honors the hungry heart every time! She was tasked with being a messenger of his resurrection to the other disciples, all because she was at the tomb looking to care for her Savior's body. What a beautiful miracle she witnessed.

Lord, as I seek you, you reveal yourself, and my witness turns into my message. Thank you!

Scripture Reading: Acts 1-3

United in Prayer

They all met together and were constantly united in prayer.

ACTS 1:14 NLT

The early church made it a priority to meet together for prayer. This is why they were so unified by it. Making prayer a practice with others is the foundation for the Spirit pouring out over us, both in the unity of love and in the power of spiritual gifts.

If we want unity, we can't ignore the power of prayer. If we want to see the Lord move in our midst, we can't neglect meeting together in the name of Christ, humbling our hearts before him and with each other. How much more does the earnest prayer of many righteous people gathering together have power to bring about the results of God's beautiful kingdom?

Righteous One, I long for a revival of your presence, not only in my own life, but in this world. I know it begins in prayer. Unite your people as we seek you.

Scripture Reading: Acts 4-6

Christlike Boldness

When they saw the boldness of Peter and John, and perceived that they were uneducated, common men, they were astonished. And they recognized that they had been with Jesus.

ACTS 4:13 ESV

Peter and John didn't have any education that should have made them confident or wise as they spoke in front of the high priest. The religious leaders were astonished by the boldness of their speech, and the fruit of their words revealed who they had been with—Jesus. Jesus was their teacher, and it was clear that they were disciples.

When we become followers of Christ, making his ways our own and putting his wisdom into practice, we too reflect his likeness. The boldness of Peter and John to stand on the law of Christ's love rather than fall in line with the religious elite is our invitation even today. The more we know Christ, the more we are changed by him, and with that comes confidence to stand.

Savior, you are worthy of my trust and my allegiance.

Scripture Reading: Acts 7-9

On Our Way

Those who were scattered went on their way preaching the word.

ACTS 8:4 CSB

Even in the aftermath of pain, even when we are forced to leave where we had made ourselves at home, we can go forth with purpose. Christ goes with us, and we can go on our way preaching the powerful Word of his redemption.

Redirection happens many different ways in life. Sometimes we choose it. Sometimes it chooses us. As we transition, let's go with the power of the gospel as our message and the presence of the Holy Spirit as our guide. We can be sure that no matter where we go, God's love is right there with us.

Lord, you are my help and guide in every season. I will praise your name through all of it.

Scripture Reading: Acts 10-12

Same Gift

"If God gave them the same gift as He also gave to us after believing in the Lord Jesus Christ, who was I that I could stand in God's way?"

ACTS 11:17 NASB

Jesus offers the same gift, the same saving grace, to all who believe in him as their Lord and Savior. Who are we to stand in the way of someone receiving his mercy? May we be conduits of his grace and generous with the gospel of peace.

When we start to believe that there are some suited to receive the kindness of God and some who don't deserve it, we lose hold of the message of the gospel.

Lord Jesus, help me to remain humble before you. I want to rejoice with heaven when the lost are found, the captives set free, and the sick are healed in your powerful name.

Scripture Reading: Acts 13-15

Called and Commissioned

The Holy Spirit said, "Now separate to Me Barnabas and Saul for the work to which I have called them." Then, having fasted and prayed, and laid hands on them, they sent them away.

ACTS 13:2-3 NKJV

In prayer, the Holy Spirit spoke that Barnabas and Saul (Paul) were to be set apart and sent out to spread the message of Christ. They were missionaries before anyone knew what that was. They were called, commissioned, and sent out.

It is powerful to be commissioned for God's work. Through prayer and the laying on of hands, we agree with God's call and pray for his Spirit to carry them into the work that he has laid out for them. We pray for direction, protection, and clarity. And we pray for power and truth to pour forth from hearts filled with love.

Holy Spirit, I choose to partner with you. You are worthy!

Scripture Reading: Acts 16-18

Praise to Breakthrough

Suddenly, there was a strong earthquake that shook the foundation of the jail. Then all the doors of the jail broke open, and all the prisoners were freed from their chains.

ACTS 16:26 NCV

Prayer and singing paved the way for prison doors to be opened miraculously. Not only were Paul and Barnabas commissioned and sent out, but they were devoted to the Lord and trusted that even after being put in prison, God was worthy of their praise.

Let's praise our way to breakthrough. When unexpected challenges arise, let's not give up hope. Let's not look at what we could have done differently. As long as we're following the Lord, we are on the path of his miraculous love.

Jesus, you are worthy of my prayers and praises, no matter where I am or what is going on. I worship you in the hard times, knowing you haven't changed a bit.

Scripture Reading: Acts 19-21

Count It as Loss

I consider my life worth nothing to me; my only aim is to finish the race and complete the task the Lord Jesus has given me—the task of testifying to the good news of God's grace.

ACTS 20:24 NIV

Paul was willing to follow the Lord even when it meant he would suffer. He counted his life a worthy sacrifice to proclaim the power of God's mercy to all who would listen. His life, once dedicated to persecuting God's Church, was irrevocably changed. He would follow God to the end.

The good news of God's grace is worth more than we realize. It is worth more than comfort, more than wealth. It is generous, powerful, and available to all who will receive it.

Lord, it's never too late for me to give my life to you, and for that I am grateful. I want to count my life as nothing in comparison to the treasure I find in you.

Scripture Reading: Acts 22-24

Same Hope

I have the same hope in God that these men have, that he will raise both the righteous and the unrighteous. Because of this, I always try to maintain a clear conscience before God and all people.

ACTS 24:15-16 NLT

Jesus is the great unifier of faith. He is the hope that holds us together. Confident hope comes in a place of faith-filled trust. This is what Paul demonstrated before the Sanhedrin.

We maintain a clear conscience before God and people by walking in the love of Christ and the truth of his ways. We choose honesty over corruption, grace over bitterness, compassion over judgment, and humble hearts over arrogant attitudes. God helps us as we yield our lives to him.

Lord Jesus, I want to walk in the light of your truth and stay close to the hope of your eternal promise. You are my holy help and my constant courage.

Scripture Reading: Acts 25-28

Both Small and Great

"To this day I have had the help that comes from God, and so I stand here testifying both to small and great."

Acts 26:22 ESV

God helps us in both small and great ways. He eases our pain and opens prison doors. He is a help to all who call on him. As we follow the Lord, we can be sure that his help is ours, both in little and big ways.

God delights in helping his people. His help might look different each time, but the gracious acts of his mercy reveal the same thing: he is a faithful help in times of trouble.

God, you are the one who helps me, so I'm looking to you for your help today. I trust in you.

Scripture Reading: Romans 1-3

Unashamed

I am not ashamed of the gospel, because it is the power of God for salvation to everyone who believes.

Romans 1:16 CSB

What does it mean to be unashamed of the gospel? Perhaps it looks like devoting ourselves to the Lord Jesus and walking in his ways, no matter what others think of us. The gospel is the power of God for salvation to everyone who believes. This gracious gift is not something to be taken for granted.

There is no room for shame in the kingdom of heaven, so let's rid ourselves of it in our pursuit of God in the here and now. Let's love him wholeheartedly and follow him wherever he leads.

Lord Jesus, I am not ashamed of your gospel, for its power saves, redeems, and sets me free. Thank you!

Scripture Reading: Romans 4-6

Full Confidence

With respect to the promise of God, he did not waver in unbelief but grew strong in faith, giving glory to God, and being fully assured that what God had promised, He was able also to perform.

Romans 4:20-21 NASB

Abraham's faith was credited to him as righteousness. Even when it didn't make sense to believe that he and Sarah would have a son in their old age, he still believed God's promises were sure. He didn't waver in unbelief.

God's faithfulness is dependent upon his nature, but our faith is credited as righteousness when we take God at his Word. Let's continue to press on in faith especially in the areas we still await a promise.

Faithful One, your promises are your Word, and your Word doesn't fail. I choose to continue to believe you for what you said you would do.

Scripture Reading: Romans 7-9

It'll Work Out

We know that all things work together for good to those who love God, to those who are the called according to His purpose.

Romans 8:28 NKJV

We don't have to know how something will work out to trust that it will. It might not be how we expected or hoped, but God's mercy is able to do far more than we can imagine. Instead of being discouraged in the face of the unknown, let's put our trust in God and remember he will work it out.

What is our part in this? It's to love God, to keep growing in grace, and to trust him along the way. As we follow him, one day we will look back and see how the thread of his mercy wove it all together with miraculous wisdom.

Lord God, I turn my heart toward you in love. I trust you on the clear days and the cloudy ones. You never change, though my understanding of you does.

Scripture Reading: Romans 10-12

Mind of Christ

Do not be shaped by this world; instead be changed within by a new way of thinking. Then you will be able to decide what God wants for you; you will know what is good and pleasing to him and what is perfect.

Romans 12:2 NCV

As we offer ourselves as living sacrifices to the Lord, he transforms us from the inside out. Instead of being shaped by the world, we are molded by the hands of the Potter. He gives us a new way of thinking. He shows us the wisdom of his ways and leads us in the light of his love.

Offering our lives to God is not a small choice on our part, and it's not an insignificant action to God. He honors our surrender with the power of his Spirit. All that he does, he does in mercy. All that he teaches is based in the wisdom of his truth. The more we surrender and follow Christ, the more clear his path becomes.

Lord, I ask for the mind of Christ that I might have a new way of thinking—your way.

Scripture Reading: Romans 13-14

One Rule

All these commands and all others are really only one rule: "Love your neighbor as you love yourself." Love never hurts a neighbor, so loving is obeying all the law.

ROMANS 13:9-10 NCV

Today's verse doubles down on what Jesus said was the whole of the law: love. Love God, love your neighbor. Love. It really does all come down to that! If we think this is too simple, we need a fresh encounter with the power of God's love. It is the very essence of who he is, and it is the highest call we have.

We can so easily get distracted by trying to do all the right things, but if we set our hearts on the most important aspect, everything else will work itself out. If we put our energy into being loving, the rest of God's kingdom traits will grow as well.

God, when I think that love isn't enough, reveal to me the expanse of it. I choose to put my effort into loving well today.

Scripture Reading: Romans 15-16

Teachable Moments

Everything that was written in the past was written to teach us, so that through the endurance taught in the Scriptures and the encouragement they provide we might have hope.

ROMANS 15:4 NIV

Endurance is necessary. Life requires us to wait, and waiting requires perseverance to keep going and not give up. There are countless times in Scripture where God's people had to wait much longer than they expected. Those who trusted God saw the fruit of the promise.

We live in a world full of convenience and instant answers. But the wisdom of God isn't found in how quickly something happens. We do well when we learn to slow down and take time. It teaches us to celebrate the pause. Let's lean into the waiting, not as an empty time where we twiddle our thumbs, but as a beautiful time of growth, of change, and of choice.

Lord, I want to learn to love the moment, and to love you in it. Teach me patience and endurance.

Scripture Reading: 1 Corinthians 1-3

Kept Blameless

He will keep you strong to the end so that you will be free from all blame on the day when our Lord Jesus Christ returns. God will do this, for he is faithful to do what he says.

1 Corinthians 1:8-9 NLT

In our weakness, we are made strong in Christ. As we lean on his grace, he pours his strength into us. God keeps us blameless as we hide ourselves in him. It's not our job to be perfect. It is our duty to stay surrendered.

God is faithful to do all he has said. As we wait for Jesus' return, let's rejoice in the time we've been given to learn to love him and others well. Let's become pursuers of peace, rivers of righteousness in a dry land, and carriers of kindness.

Lord, I keep myself in you, and you keep me strong, blameless, and righteous. Thank you.

Scripture Reading: 1 Corinthians 4-6

Powerful Kingdom

The kingdom of God does not consist in talk but in power.

1 Corinthians 4:20 ESV

All talk and little action doesn't prove much. Anyone can talk big, but those who walk in the ways of Christ have the power of faith-filled action to back them up. The Holy Spirit's power is evident in the lives of those who are devoted to the Lord.

We aren't meant to keep our faith in the realm of theory. Faith is backed up by action. It shows itself in how we live. The power of God to heal, set free, and purify is on display in his devoted lovers. May we walk in faith, and lead people to love, to grace, to wholeness, and to unifying peace.

Lord Jesus, be honored in my life and be revealed in the way I live.

Scripture Reading: 1 Corinthians 7-9

Present Transformation

Brothers and sisters, each person is to remain with God in the situation in which he was called.

1 CORINTHIANS 7:24 CSB

When God receives us and transforms our lives, it doesn't mean we have to suddenly abandon everything. With time, it will become clear what God asks us to pursue and what he asks us to leave behind. But when we don't know what to do except praise God in the present? That is enough.

Let's welcome God's transformative love to meet us where we are already planted. As we pray for his power to move, he answers by meeting us where we are and bringing seeds of his kindness through the soil of our lives. We can bloom where we're planted as the showers of his blessing rain down on us.

Lord, you change everything for the better. I invite you to be here with me.

Scripture Reading: 1 Corinthians 10-12

All for God's Glory

Whether you eat or drink, or whatever you do, do all things for the glory of God.

1 Corinthians 10:31 NASB

Everything we do can be an offering to the Lord. When we take our food with gratitude, do our work with integrity, talk to others with grace, listen to the needs of friends, serve in generous compassion—no matter what it is—it can glorify God if it's done with a heart that is surrendered to him.

Maybe you don't think about how the little things you do in life can reflect God. If that's true, today's a great opportunity to think about it as you move throughout your day.

God, I want you to be glorified in the simple things of life as well as in the big ones.f

Scripture Reading: 1 Corinthians 13-16

These Three

Now abide faith, hope, love, these three; but the greatest of these is love.

1 Corinthians 13:13 NKJV

The three things that remain when everything else falls away are faith, hope, and love. These are three important virtues to keep at the forefront of our minds, hearts, and lives.

Love hopes all things. It believes all things. It endures. If God is love, we can replace each instance of love with God in this passage. God hopes all things. He believes all things. He endures. Everything else may pass away, but he remains, and in him remain these principles. We cannot go wrong by choosing to grow in faith, hold onto hope, and live in love.

Everlasting One, I want to build my life upon you and who you are.

Scripture Reading: 2 Corinthians 1-3

All Comfort

God is the Father who is full of mercy and all comfort. He comforts us every time we have trouble, so when others have trouble, we can comfort them with the same comfort God gives us.

2 CORINTHIANS 1:3-4

Every time we have trouble, whether it's internal or external, God is close. He draws close, relieving our tension with his loving presence. He is always close to the brokenhearted and discouraged. He is close in grief and in disappointment.

Everything God does is an example of how we can be with each other. We are comforted, and we learn to comfort others. There is nothing expected of us that he does not first provide. Let's remember that the love, comfort, peace, and joy we find in him is meant to be shared with others.

Comforter, thank you for the way you meet me with the gentle and powerful peace of your presence.

Scripture Reading: 2 Corinthians 4-6

Inner Renewal

We do not lose heart. Though outwardly we are wasting away, yet inwardly we are being renewed day by day.
2 Corinthians 4:16 niv

We can't avoid challenges or troubles in this life, but that doesn't mean we have to be taken down by them. God is with us in the messes just as constantly as he is with us in the triumphs and times of ease. His Spirit offers us renewal every day.

We are never without the strength of his grace reaching us through the power of his presence. It doesn't matter what goes on around us or what we face. He is with us, and that is enough to renew us from the inside out.

Present One, it doesn't matter what comes, you are with me, and that's what matters most. With you, I am secure.

Scripture Reading: 2 Corinthians 7-9

Cycles of Generosity

God will generously provide all you need. Then you will always have everything you need and plenty left over to share with others.

2 Corinthians 9:8 NLT

Out of God's generosity, we are able to share with others. God loves a cheerful giver, and he blesses the hand that is open to help those in need. Even in generosity, we don't depend on our own strength. We give out of the overflow of God's goodness!

It is a choice to be generous or to withhold. May we follow in the lead of our loving Savior, holding nothing back from those who ask. May we have wisdom, discernment, and grace as our foundation. Let's stretch our giving muscles today.

Generous One, you are more gracious than anyone I've known. I want to resemble you in generosity.

Scripture Reading: 2 Corinthians 10-13

Strength in Weakness

"My grace is sufficient for you, for my power is made perfect in weakness." Therefore I will boast all the more gladly of my weaknesses, so that the power of Christ may rest upon me… For when I am weak, then I am strong.

2 Corinthians 12:9-10 esv

God's grace meets us in our weakest moments and offers us his strength. We don't have to rely on our own to represent him. In fact, his powerful presence reveals itself more readily through our weakness.

Let's not avoid God in our messy moments. That is when we need him most! He is faithful to draw near in kindness and to empower us with his strength. He doesn't love us any more on our good days. He doesn't expect any more of us on our weakest. Let's lean into him, and rely on his presence, for that is what he wants most.

Lord, you offer me the grace of your strength in my weakness. Be glorified in me, as I surrender to you.

Scripture Reading: Galatians 1-3

God Pleaser

Am I now trying to persuade people, or God? Or am I striving to please people? If I were still trying to please people, I would not be a servant of Christ.

Galatians 1:10 csb

People-pleasing is a trap that women easily fall into. Because we can anticipate what others need so often, we try to keep the peace by anticipating what others might think of us. Instead of living in the freedom of God's love, we end up shrinking ourselves to please others.

We were made for more than fitting in, being palatable, and soothing others' egos. Let's walk in the light of God's truth, and put his ways first. As we abandon ourselves to his love, he invites us to walk more fully in his freedom for his pleasure and not for the expectations of others.

Lord, I don't want to shrink myself by trying to appease others when it goes against the very core of who you've called me to be. I choose your approval today.

Scripture Reading: Galatians 4-6

Spiritual Fruit

The fruit of the Spirit is love, joy, peace, patience, kindness, goodness, faithfulness, gentleness, self-control; against such things there is no law.

GALATIANS 5:22-23 NASB

The fruit of the Spirit reveals God's work in our lives. It doesn't mean we always react correctly. We all have moments of impatience, bitterness, worry, or loss of control. God's fruit is much more lasting than the chaos of a moment.

If we look at the larger arc of our lives—our relationships, work ethic, and reputation—we can see the fruit that's showing up. As we yield our hearts to the Lord and allow his powerful love to transform us, his fruit makes itself known in our actions.

Holy Spirit, may your fruit become more evident in my life as I follow the ways of Christ.

Scripture Reading: Ephesians 1-3

Exceeding Greatness

That you may know what is the hope of His calling… what is the exceeding greatness of His power toward us who believe, according to the working of His mighty power.

EPHESIANS 1:18-19 NKJV

Do you know the hope of your calling in Christ? Have the eyes of your heart been opened to the exceeding greatness of his power toward you? This is the prayer that Paul opened this letter with, and it's a powerful prayer that reaches through the ages to cover every believer.

Following Christ is not just a safe bet, it is the path to abundant life. We get to experience his goodness over and over again as we trust him and lean on his wisdom. May you know the expansive love of Christ which passes all knowledge.

Lord, expand my understanding of your love, your wisdom, and your goodness today.

Scripture Reading: Ephesians 4-6

Live It Out

I urge you who have been chosen by God to live up to the life to which God called you. Always be humble, gentle, and patient, accepting each other in love.

EPHESIANS 4:1-2 NCV

Paul wrote this letter from a prison cell. He wasn't bitter about where he was; he only wanted to encourage others to live in a way that honored God, empowered by surrender to his Spirit. Living out God's love is not complicated. It isn't always an easy choice, but it is simple.

Choosing humble hearts, gentle approaches, patience in the waiting, and accepting each other in love reveals the power of Christ at work within our hearts. It is much easier to let walls of self-protection keep us in gilded cages of pride. But this is not the way of Christ. Humility, gentleness, and patience reveal the power of God's mercy at work within us.

Lord, when I'm tempted to harden my heart in pride, protection, or indifference, help me to choose the better way.

Scripture Reading: Philippians 1-4

God's Work

He who began a good work in you will carry it on to completion until the day of Christ Jesus… for it is God who works in you to will and to act in order to fulfill his good purpose.

PHILIPPIANS 1:6, 2:13 NIV

It is God who works in us to will and to act in ways that fulfill his good purpose. When we surrender our hearts and lives to him, he does the important work. Transformation begins in our hearts and minds, and it trickles into our actions as we put his law of love into practice.

Let's not get so caught up in what we're doing well or poorly that we forget it is God's strength that helps us in all things. It is his work that was begun when we came to Christ. As we partner with his purposes, he continues to transform us in his likeness.

Lord, it is your good work that was started in me, and I trust you to carry it on until its completion.

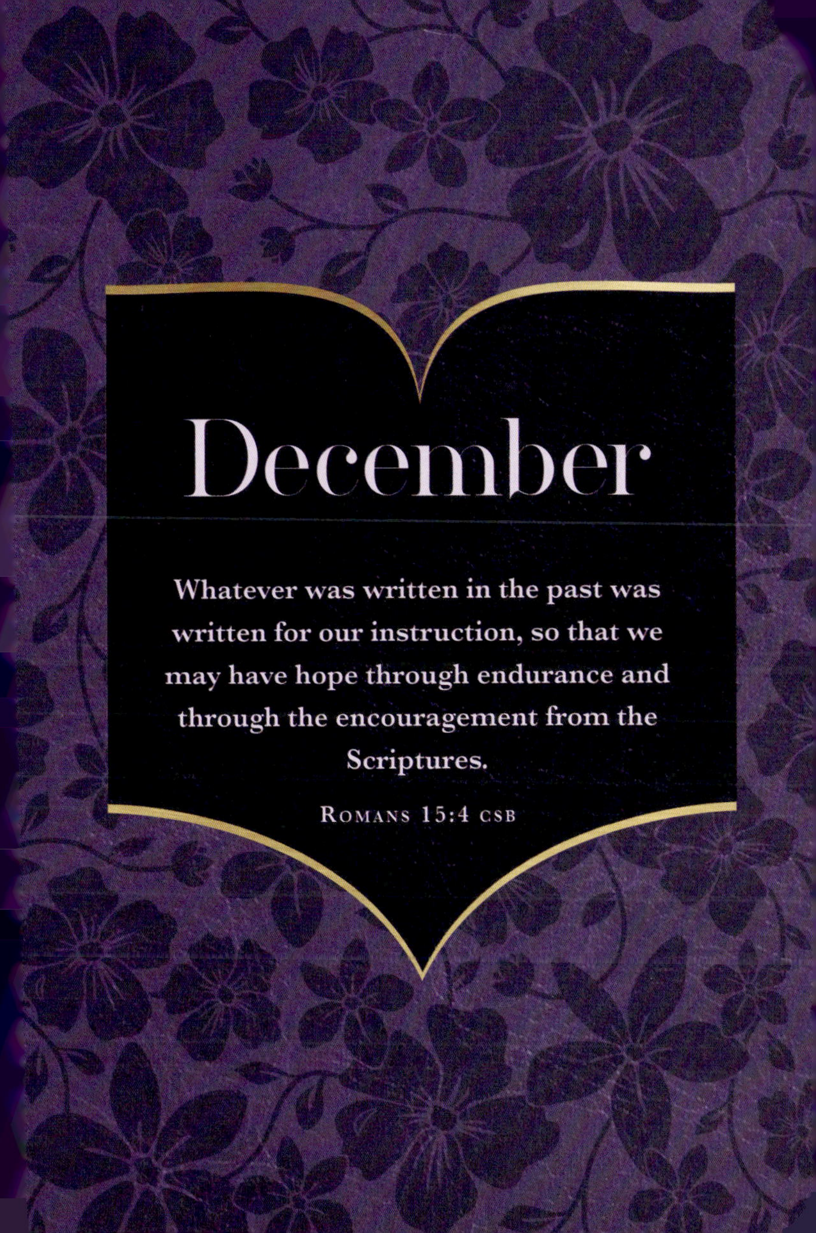
December
Whatever was written in the past was written for our instruction, so that we may have hope through endurance and through the encouragement from the Scriptures.
Romans 15:4 CSB

Scripture Reading: Colossians 1-4

Realities of Peace

Set your sights on the realities of heaven, where Christ sits in the place of honor at God's right hand. Think about the things of heaven, not the things of earth. And let the peace that comes from Christ rule in your hearts.

COLOSSIANS 3:1-2,15 NLT

When we set our minds on heavenly things instead of being consumed by earthly problems, we shift our perspective from the temporary to the eternal. What are the things that will last? Are they not faith, hope, and love? The peace of God is meant to keep our minds and hearts at rest no matter what is going on around us.

We can know the power of God's peace in our midst every moment of every day. Peace is our portion, and it is a heavenly gift. Let's fix our gaze on the Prince of Peace today.

Everlasting One, your ways are not influenced by the chaos of this world. You remain steadfast and true. I choose to set my heart upon you today.

Scripture Reading: 1 Thessalonians 1-3

Increase and Abound

May the Lord make you increase and abound in love for one another and for all, as we do for you, so that he may establish your hearts blameless.

1 Thessalonians 3:12-13 ESV

If it wasn't already clear, love is the foundation and highest aim of all we do in this life. It is love that formed us, and it is love that saved us. It is love that leads us, and love that pursues us still. When we become conduits of God's love, it flows in and through us.

Love is not static or fixed. It is a force that increases and multiplies as we use it. It is more than a feeling, and it's also more than a choice. May we set our hearts on growing in love each day, looking for ways to show it to the people around us.

Lord of love, I surrender to you. Make your love increase and abound in me as I spread it like seeds in this world.

Scripture Reading: 1 Thessalonians 4-5

God's Will

Rejoice always, pray constantly, give thanks in everything; for this is God's will for you in Christ Jesus.

1 THESSALONIANS 5:16-18 CSB

If God's will for us is that we rejoice always, pray constantly, and give thanks, we shouldn't be at a loss for what to offer him today. His will isn't cryptic. He guides us in truth and in love, and he is much more concerned with *how* we live than what exactly we do. We can invite him into our work, rejoicing in his present grace, praying throughout our day, and giving thanks in all things.

God's will is not complicated. He is able to do far more than we can imagine with the little faith we offer him. Instead of worrying over whether we're doing the right thing, let's focus on doing what this verse encourages: rejoicing, praying, and giving thanks.

Lord, you are worthy of my attention. That is what I offer you today. You have my heart, my gratitude, and my ear. Have your way as I move through this day rejoicing in your nearness.

Scripture Reading: 2 Thessalonians 1-3

Faithful Peace

The Lord is faithful, and He will strengthen and protect you from the evil one.

2 THESSALONIANS 3:3 NASB

There is nothing to fear when we put God at the head of our lives. He is faithful to strengthen and protect us. No one can snatch us from his hand. His grip of grace is sure! May we know the powerful peace and confident courage of following after him, for he never abandons us.

As Paul later prayed, "May the Lord of peace himself continually grant you peace in every circumstance" (verse sixteen). There's absolutely no situation where we are without access to his peace! It is the peace that passes all understanding and strengthens our courage when fear rises.

Lord, you keep me close and protect me. I trust you to do what I can't and to keep me at rest in situations I couldn't foresee.

Scripture Reading: 1 Timothy 1-3

Our Mediator

There is one God and one Mediator between God and men, the Man Christ Jesus, who gave Himself a ransom for all, to be testified in due time.

1 TIMOTHY 2:5-6 NKJV

Jesus Christ is our mediator. He went before the Father, making himself the go-between in glory and grace. There is no one more worthy to plead our case before God, or to present us as a people purified by his redemptive sacrifice. He is the door to the Father, and he welcomes us every time we approach him.

If Christ is our mediator, why would we waste our time trying to find favor with God through any other means? The gift of grace is available to all. We can trust him to be a faithful witness and powerful redeemer.

Redeemer, you are the one who pleads my case before the Father. By your blood, I am cleansed, liberated, and made right. Thank you!

Scripture Reading: 1 Timothy 4-6

Easy to See

Good deeds are easy to see, but even those that are not easily seen cannot stay hidden.

1 Timothy 5:25 NCV

We don't have to look hard to see goodness. Good deeds are easy to spot, and they offer encouragement, peace, kindness, and more to those on both the receiving and giving ends.

Goodness cannot stay hidden. It will be uncovered. Why not spread it through our lives like seeds, waiting for them to bloom and catch people off-guard? If we truly knew the power of kindness, we wouldn't hesitate to offer it freely. Let's become people who do good, not for recognition but for the joy of watching goodness unfold in this world.

Good God, I want to grow in grace, in generosity, and in kindness. Enlighten my creativity as I look for ways to sow goodness into the world around me.

Scripture Reading: 2 Timothy 1-4

Boldness

The Spirit God gave us does not make us timid, but gives us power, love and self-discipline.

2 TIMOTHY 1:7 NIV

The Spirit of God doesn't make us hesitant, he makes us bold. There is power in his presence, love to fill and fuel us, and self-discipline to make grounded, wise choices. God's Spirit enhances every good thing we could do on our own.

Though some expect women to be timid, God never asks that. He gives us as much boldness and courage as he does anyone else. Galatians 3:8 assures us there is no distinction between people in God's kingdom. As part of a unified body, women can be powerful, disciplined, and loving.

Spirit of God, you are the one who gives me boldness and courage to stand. I will not shrink when others expect it. I will remain strong in you.

Scripture Reading: Titus 1-3

Confident Assurance

He generously poured out the Spirit upon us through Jesus Christ our Savior. Because of his grace he made us right in his sight and gave us confidence that we will inherit eternal life.

TITUS 3:6-7 NLT

The confidence of eternal life has nothing to do with us and everything to do with Jesus Christ. Our salvation is based in his grace, a gift that we could never earn or lose, and it is our confidence. In Christ, we have become children of God, no matter where we came from or what we did before.

What are you most sure of in this life? Does your salvation make the list? God wants you to know the power of his love as it moves you from death to life, from shame to freedom, and from fear to peace. Join your life with Christ, and you can stand unafraid, unashamed, and fully convinced of your place in his kingdom.

Lord Jesus, you are my confidence. In you I am made new, and I stand upon what you say is true.

Scripture Reading: Philemon 1

Express Your Gratitude

I thank my God always when I remember you in my prayers… For I have derived much joy and comfort from your love.

PHILEMON 1:4,7 ESV

If we don't intentionally take time to express gratitude to those who bless us, we miss out on the opportunity to build each other up in love. Gratitude is a powerful expression, not only toward God but toward the people in our lives who make a difference.

The people who bring joy and comfort, the ones who show up when it matters most, we are lucky to know them! Let's not overlook the importance of expressing our gratitude, and encouraging them.

Lord, thank you for the people who reflect your kindness in my life. I won't hold back from expressing my love and gratitude toward them.

Scripture Reading: Hebrews 1-3

Today's Invitation

Encourage each other daily, while it is still called today, so that none of you is hardened by sin's deception.

HEBREWS 3:13 CSB

As we encourage each other in loving support, in the power of the Spirit, and in perseverance, we strengthen and build each other up to stay connected to each other and to the Lord.

As long as it is called today, this is our holy responsibility. We don't ever have to walk this road of life alone, and we surely aren't meant to. In the body of believers, we are strengthened. As we pray for one another, encourage each other, and call each other up in truth, we grow together in the goodness and power of God.

Lord, today I choose to take every opportunity I have to encourage others in love, in truth, and in pursuit of you.

Scripture Reading: Hebrews 4-6

The Anchor Holds

This hope we have as an anchor of the soul, a hope both sure and reliable and one which enters within the veil, where Jesus has entered as a forerunner for us.

HEBREWS 6:19-20 NASB

Jesus Christ is our living hope. He is the one who goes before us into the throne room of the Father, the one who ushers us into the kingdom of God. Our anchor of hope is secure, so let's keep our hearts tethered to that steady weight through prayerful trust.

God will not fail us. Christ has not abandoned us or left us to our own devices. We have the Spirit of truth, the holy helper, who keeps us steady. Our anchor of hope remains rooted in Christ.

Lord, no matter how the winds of this world shift, my anchor is firmly in you. You hold me steady, even when the storms rage. Thank you.

Scripture Reading: Hebrews 7-9

Heavenly Intercessor

He is also able to save to the uttermost those who come to God through Him, since He always lives to make intercession for them.

HEBREWS 7:25 NKJV

God saves us completely and thoroughly. We can trust him. All who come to Christ are received wholeheartedly. Not only that, but he lives to make intercession for us. In plain speak, that means Christ prays for us.

How does it make you feel to know that Christ is praying for you right now? He is interceding for you as you turn your heart toward him. It is too wonderful to comprehend, and too lofty for the mind to make sense of, but Jesus prays constantly for you. Knowing that, can you trust him more today?

Lord Jesus, thank you for thinking of me. You want what is best even more than I do. I yield to you today.

Scripture Reading: Hebrews 10-13

Hold Firm

Let us hold firmly to the hope that we have confessed,
because we can trust God to do what he promised.

HEBREWS 10:23 NCV

God is a promise keeper. He always follows through on his Word. Knowing this, we can hold firmly to the hope we have in Christ. He will continue to meet us.

It requires courage to keep going. If we do, persisting in courage and choosing to keep following the ways of the Lord, we hold firmly to the hope that remains steady before us.

Lord, I know I can trust you to do what you promised, and it is that confidence that keeps me going. Strengthen my courage and increase my strength to persevere in this life and its challenges.

Scripture Reading: James 1-3

Pure Joy

Consider it pure joy, my brothers and sisters, whenever you face trials of many kinds, because you know that the testing of your faith produces perseverance. Let perseverance finish its work so that you may be mature and complete, not lacking anything.

James 1:2-4 NIV

Trials aren't a sign we're doing things wrong. They are a part of this life, and we can embrace them as readily in our faith as we do times of peace. Times of testing lead us to stronger character as we continue to welcome each obstacle as an opportunity to grow in faith.

This requires a mindset shift, but a what a shift it makes within us! Our belief systems are tied to our expectations. If we believe that trials mean we're doing things wrong, we'll resist them. If instead we look at them as opportunities for growth, we will learn to meet them as challenges to learn from.

Lord, help me to consider trials as joy, as opportunities to grow in grace, in courage, and in persistent faith.

Scripture Reading: James 4-5

Draw Near

Humble yourselves before God. Resist the devil, and he will flee from you. Come close to God, and God will come close to you.

JAMES 4:7-8 NLT

As we draw near to God, we do it with humble hearts. As we submit our hearts to him, we resist the fear, temptation, and shame of the enemy. As we do that, the feelings flee. Scripture promises that as we come close to God, he also comes close to us.

Even just a slight turn of our attention in humble openness leads us to the presence of God. He is closer than we realized. Let's take this opportunity, right here and now, to turn our attention toward our loving God and be met by his amazing grace.

Lord, I draw near to you with a heart that is humble and hands that are open in surrender. Meet me in this place with your powerful presence.

Scripture Reading: 1 Peter 1-3

Chosen

You are a chosen race, a royal priesthood, a holy nation, a people for his own possession, that you may proclaim the excellencies of him who called you out of darkness into his marvelous light.

1 PETER 2:9 ESV

We were not only chosen by God to be his children, but we were chosen out of love! In Christ, we have found a home. It is not something he offered lightly or begrudgingly. He longs for us to know him. He longs for others to answer his call.

We have been brought out of the darkness into the marvelous light. There is no shadow in Christ, and there is nothing he needs to hide from us. He is pure in his motivations, miraculous in his mercy, and generous with his peace. We have been chosen, and he won't change his mind.

Lord, thank you for choosing me as your daughter, not only to know and love you, but to be transformed by your mercy all the days of my life.

Scripture Reading: 1 Peter 4-5

Cast It All

Casting all your cares on him, because he cares about you.

1 Peter 5:7 CSB

You can give every whisper of worry, every tinge of doubt, each weight of disappointment to God without a second thought. He is kind. He's not waiting with disapproval in his gaze. He has peace to settle your anxious mind. He has clarity to clear the fog of confusion. He has love to assure you of your place in his heart.

With that in mind, will you do as this verse suggests? Cast *all* your cares on him, for he cares for you. Cast every single one: the little, the big, and the muddled things you can't even name. He is able to settle you in his peace.

Lord, I cast every care upon you today, bringing every bit of worry to you. Settle my mind, heart, and body in your perfect peace.

Scripture Reading: 2 Peter 1-3

So Very Patient

The Lord is not slow about His promise, as some count slowness, but is patient toward you, not willing for any to perish, but for all to come to repentance.

2 PETER 3:9 NASB

All that God said you can count on him doing. Sometimes we get tripped up in the timing of it. Abraham and Sarah were promised an heir, and that took longer than either of them expected. The Israelites were delivered from Egypt only to spend forty years in the wilderness before entering into the Promised Land.

Just because it's taking longer than expected doesn't mean we misunderstood God. Faith is required in the waiting, and perseverance is necessary. We can trust God to do all he has promised, and to give us strength in the waiting.

Lord, I don't want to lose sight of your faithfulness in my own waiting Make me more like you today.

Scripture Reading: 1 John 1-3

Loving Action

Let us not love in word or in tongue, but in deed and in truth. And by this we know that we are of the truth, and shall assure our hearts before Him.

1 JOHN 3:18-19 NKJV

Love is revealed in deed and in truth. Faith-filled action reveals our belief about God. When we walk in his love, we don't just say we love God. We live it love out. Jesus is the truth, and he is the living embodiment of God's love. In him, we are free!

This means we're also free to follow in his footsteps. Lots of talk with little follow-through reveals a disconnect between what we say we believe and what we actually believe. If we love in word, but we lash out in bitterness, this is not love at all. May we measure our love by our actions, and ask the Lord to motivate our actions with his lifegiving love!

Lord, I don't want to just say I love you. I want it to be clear in the way I live my life.

Scripture Reading: 1 John 4-5

Perfect Love

Where God's love is, there is no fear, because God's perfect love drives out fear. It is punishment that makes a person fear, so love is not made perfect in the person who fears.

1 John 4:18 NCV

There is no reason to fear in God's perfect love. Where we are stuck in fight, flight, or freeze, we need a fresh encounter with God's love. Fear is hasty; it pushes us to make quick decisions based in self-protection. But God's love? It expands and allows for us to slow down, see more clearly, and move with grounded action.

We don't have to be afraid of punishment when we come to the Lord. In Christ our sins are forgiven, and our shame is covered. What was hidden in the shadows is brought out into the light, and nothing is as scary when it is seen clearly. May we go to the Lord and receive his perfect love, especially when we feel fear's grip closing in.

Perfect Love, you shine, and darkness flees. Shine on me today!

Scripture Reading: 2 John 1

Walk in Love

This is love: that we walk in obedience to his commands. As you have heard from the beginning, his command is that you walk in love.

2 JOHN 1:6 NIV

Love is revealed in honor. We honor God by obeying his law of love. He is trustworthy, true, and full of goodness. There is nothing devious or hidden in his motives. Why wouldn't we willingly follow his way? There is none better!

All God wants of us is to walk in love. That is the crux of the gospel message and the whole of the law summed up. We are to love God wholeheartedly with our minds, souls, and lives and love others as we love ourselves. To walk in love is to walk in the ways of God.

Lord of Love, I don't know why I complicate what you desire or require. I humble myself in love before you, and I choose to obey your ways because you are trustworthy, faithful, and always good.

Scripture Reading: 3 John 1

Follow Goodness

Follow only what is good. Remember that those who do good prove that they are God's children, and those who do evil prove that they do not know God.

3 John 1:11 NLT

It is right to follow goodness. Goodness exemplifies God's love, his peace, and his unifying grace. It is kind, encouraging, and it supports those who serve. When we walk in love, we refuse to follow the divisive ways of those who want to be right. The humble leader is the leader who most looks like Christ.

Goodness and love follow those who seek the Lord. But this can also be reversed. As we follow goodness and unfailing love, we align ourselves with the nature of God.

Good God, I don't want to be influenced by those who only care for their own purposes and plans. Open my eyes to see those I can stand with in unifying love.

Scripture Reading: Jude 1

Called and Kept

To those who are called, beloved in God the Father and kept for Jesus Christ: May mercy, peace, and love be multiplied to you.

JUDE 1:1-2 ESV

All who are in the family of Christ are called, beloved, and kept. Not one of us is outside his mercy or too far from his grace at any time. There is mercy, peace, and love that can be multiplied in any moment.

Where we have questioned our place in Christ, or where we have believed there is a limit to what he's willing to do, may we experience the overwhelming goodness of his generous nature. He has called us, not only his own, but beloved. He loves us well, and he loves us thoroughly.

God, you have called me and will keep me in perfect peace.

Scripture Reading: Revelation 1-3

Alive Forever

"Don't be afraid. I am the First and the Last, and the Living One. I was dead, but look—I am alive forever and ever, and I hold the keys of death and Hades."

REVELATION 1:17-18 CSB

Jesus holds the keys to death because he defeated the grave. He is alive today, for he rose from the grave in resurrection power. In his redemption, we are alive too! There is no reason to fear the saving grace of our Redeemer.

One day, we will stand before God and see him as plain as we do anything else. Let's not give into the temptation to doubt his life now, for the fruit of his presence is everywhere, and it is real. We have the Spirit of truth testifying to the life of Christ within us, just as Jesus told us we would in John 14:17.

Lord Jesus, I believe that you are alive because you've transformed my life. I long for the day I'll see you with these eyes, but until then I look with eyes of faith.

Scripture Reading: Revelation 4-6

Worthy Jesus

"Worthy are You, our Lord and our God, to receive glory and honor and power; for You created all things, and because of Your will they existed, and were created."

REVELATION 4:11 NASB

Jesus, the once baby in a manger who grew in wisdom and stature and offered his life for all who would believe in him, is the one who is worthy of all praise. He is the Son of God, Emmanuel, and the glorious one we lift high and honor today.

The Son of God became the Son of Man and walked among us. He was humble, not thinking himself above any other, though he walked in the confidence of God's power and love. This beautiful King is the one who reigns forever. Let's worship him in spirit and in truth as we pour out our hearts in thanksgiving today.

Lord Jesus, thank you for humbling yourself to the human experience, and for bringing us back to the Father.

Scripture Reading: Revelation 7-9

Great Multitude

A great multitude which no one could number, of all nations, tribes, peoples, and tongues, standing before the throne and before the Lamb, clothed with white robes, with palm branches in their hands.

REVELATION 7:9 NKJV

If you want a glimpse of what heaven will look like, this is a great verse to sum it up. A great multitude, filled with people from every nation, tribe, people, and dialect, standing before the throne of the Lamb. This is Christ's own special people.

We can't imagine how wonderfully diverse Christ's kingdom is, and yet we can catch glimpses of it on the earth. Any time people of all different types of backgrounds come together in unity and love to worship and serve him, we see a tiny glimpse of what it will be like in the fullness of that glorious day!

Lord, you have created such a beautiful variety of people, and they all belong in your kingdom. I worship you today in great expectation of what it will be like one day.

Scripture Reading: Revelation 10-12

Powerful Promises

He made a promise by the power of the One who lives forever and ever. He is the One who made the skies and all that is in them, the earth and all that is in it, and the sea and all that is in it.

REVELATION 10:6 NCV

In Jesus' name promises were made and kept, and they are still. Let's follow the lead of heaven and not promise by heaven or by earth, but by the one who created them. It's important to know what's worthy of a promise.

Jesus knew the power of covenants. When we make a promise in the name of the Lord, it is not to be taken lightly. It must be something we are absolutely sure of without a shadow of a doubt. Let's keep things simple and cling to his promises. God's power is greater than any other, and he does no wrong. We can trust him.

Lord, instead of making promises I can't keep, I will cling to your promises that can't fail.

Scripture Reading: Revelation 13-15

Patient Endurance

This calls for patient endurance on the part of the people of God who keep his commands and remain faithful to Jesus.

REVELATION 14:12 NIV

Blessed are we to stand strong in the Lord and keep following him. Faith keeps us moving forward in him, and he keeps us with the power of his love. Standing strong doesn't mean always feeling strong. We can do all things through Christ who gives us strength, including being patient in endurance, keeping his commands, and remaining faithful to his Word.

Our deeds from this life follow us. When we choose to remain in the Lord, his love remains in us even into the next age. We cannot escape his goodness, and the good we do in his name will not be forgotten. What reason to continue to patiently endure and remain faithful to our Savior!

Lord, I know how I live matters. May I have patience to continue on your path of love as you lead me.

Scripture Reading: Revelation 16-18

Rejoice in Justice

Rejoice over her fate, O heaven
and people of God and apostles and prophets!
For at last God has judged her
for your sakes.

REVELATION 18:20 NLT

God's justice will come, and it will be full of his truth and power. God will make all wrong things right, and he will settle all disputes in the power of his just measurements. We can trust him to do it.

Let's give up the need to judge others here and now, and do what Christ has called us to: to love others with our lives. It's God's job to judge, for he sees everything clearly and without partiality. He is able to do what none of us can, and we can trust him to set everything straight in his perfect timing.

Righteous Judge, no one can make the judgments you do. I give up the right to revenge and bitterness and humble my heart in love.

Scripture Reading: Revelation 19-20

The Lord Almighty Reigns

Then I heard what seemed to be the voice of a great multitude, like the roar of many waters and like the sound of mighty peals of thunder, crying out,

"Hallelujah!
For the Lord our God
the Almighty reigns."

REVELATION 19:6 ESV

What a time of worship and celebration it will be as we stand before the throne singing to our Lord God Almighty. He deserves all the glory and honor, and we don't have to wait until the roar reaches our own ears to join in.

Let's move our hearts in worship and wonder before the King of Kings and Lord of Lords today.

Lord Almighty, I'm not waiting another moment to worship you. I join my voice with those in the earth and in heaven and sing: Hallelujah! You reign!

Scripture Reading: Revelation 21-22

Glorious Hope

He will wipe away every tear from their eyes. Death will be no more; grief, crying, and pain will be no more, because the previous things have passed away.

REVELATION 21:4 CSB

Oh, we look forward to the promised day of God's kingdom coming to earth in fullness. What we experience now in losses, grief, and sacrifice, will turn to memory in the light of God's glorious kingdom. He will wipe every tear, removing our grief, death, pain, and suffering.

As we await that day with glorious hope, let's celebrate the goodness of God with us now. His peace is persistent. His grace is generous. His mercy is miraculous. The love of God cannot be quenched, and his wisdom will never fail. One day, everything will be set right and worshiping the Lord will no longer be a sacrifice. It will be as natural as breathing.

Lord, you have led me through your Word with the power of your presence. I choose to offer myself to you each day, holding onto hope and following your path of love. You are my God, and I worship you.

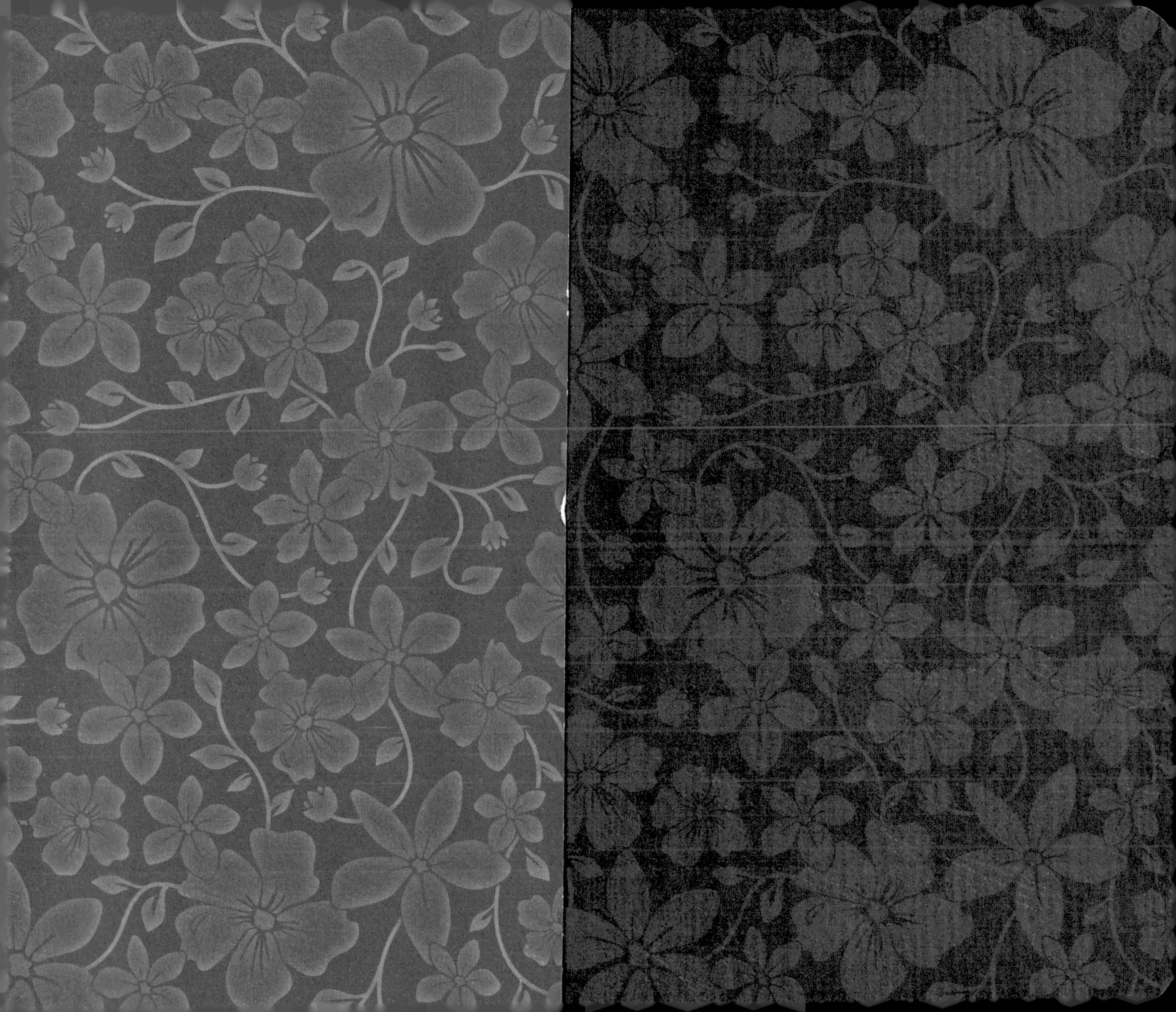